Trans/substantiation
The Metaphysics of Transgender

Alan McManus

COPYRIGHT

First published in Scotland
Feast of *Corpus Christi*, 2017

ISBN-13: 978-1548111700
ISBN-10: 1548111708

DEDICATION

To Ian, who opened up a whole new world to me, and to all whose voice is marginalised.

THANKS

To trans and feminist friends, Roman Catholics and Reformed Christians who have shared their experiences and beliefs with me. To my mother for cheering company and for the benefit of her professional knowledge as a State Registered Nurse and Midwife. And for her wise words on cats. To Ciaran, Mhairi, Clare, Joe and Pat for insightful discussion and feedback on drafts. To Gavin and John for hospitality and hilarity. Thanks also to Piotr Siedlecki who has released his photo, 'White Snowflake 2', into the Public Domain on: www.publicdomainpictures.net

CONTENTS

Hoc est corpus meum.
['This is my body']

(Latin words of consecration)

Our Bodies, Our Selves!

(Second Wave feminist slogan)

You put your whole self in,
your whole self out
In out, in out,
shake it all about!
You do the Hokey Cokey
and you turn around
That's what it's all about!
O Hokey Cokey Cokey!
O Hokey Cokey Cokey!
O Hokey Cokey Cokey!
Knees bend, hands up
Raa raa raa!

(Traditional folksong with actions)

Our Bodies, Our Souls

(Naomi Wolf)[1]

---

[1] Title of Wolf/1995.

Introduction

This book is made up of two parts. The first is a fairly conventionally-written essay in the style of critical theory and modern theology; the second is a short story which is at once a gift-of-sale, a thank-you for getting through the page upon page of philosophical considerations, and an illustration (by no means a recommendation!) of a different way to perform gender relations. Although based, transparently, on Plato's *Republic*, it is not meant to be dystopian and is only utopian in the literal sense of being located nowhere (on Earth). I hope you enjoy it and it provides fruitful meditation on the thoughts put forward in the first part of the book, which I now introduce.

Sexual politics gets very personal as radical second wave feminists raise fears about persons with penises in female public toilets; midwives are instructed that the word 'mother' is discriminatory to pregnant trans men; and transactivists relate their experience of exclusion from female space and feminist solidarity. Queer theory has led to the umbrella term 'transgender' being used for transsexual and transvestite people alike, and sometimes also to genderqueer or non-binary people who are not necessarily people with an intersex trait. Gender is also the basis of religious conflict over ministry and sexual ethics and the centuries-old pious but acrimonious debate on the reality and mode of change and presence, in the Christian ritual of Holy Communion, continues without resolution.

What these two debates have in common is that on one side of each there is an assertion of a reality inaccessible to, and independent of, the evidence of the five human senses; on the other side of each there is an assertion of the distinction between symbol, similarity and identity.

The difference lies in the nature of the assertion. Catholics who believe in transubstantiation (that bread and wine become only body and blood) use the mediaeval language of scholasticism to explain their belief in this mystical change and presence. In contrast, some transactivists do not put forward their assertion (that a man can undergo a transition and become a woman, retroactively, or *vice-versa*) as a belief but as a fact that must be accepted irrespective of any lack of medical evidence and irreducible to personal psychology.

Whereas Catholics consider those who do not accept their assertion to be lacking in faith, but not necessarily in goodwill or intelligence, transactivists accuse their doubters of transphobia and while respecting their right to free speech, deny them a platform to exercise it.

Noting that Catholics are not committed to any particular language in which to express this assertion,[2] I offer a new interpretation of change and presence – one that may also be helpful to those engaged in debate over transgender. This interpretation concerns ontology, the academic discipline of being or 'the nature of nature'.[3] This is a word very much in vogue with Queer theorists such as Judith Butler, whose book *Gender Trouble* focussed feminist debate on the social construction of not only gender but of sex itself. Another, older, word for the nature of nature, used by Aristotle's editor, is 'metaphysics' – a word derided by most mainstream philosophers and critical theorists as it smacks of spirituality and God-talk.

---

[2] Sokolowski/2006/15 references the insistence of Pope John Paul II on this point in his 1998 Encyclical, *Fides et Ratio* (Faith and Reason).
[3] See McManus/2013/Ch.4.

This derision is unfortunate as many modern critical theorists, by their chosen ignorance of the venerable tradition of this academic discipline, are left in the position of attempting to reinvent the wheel – and have created some patent absurdities in the process.[4] Umberto Eco notes that the philosophical and semiotic issues raised by post-structuralism and postmodernism were debated by mediaeval scholastics – so critical theorists may find that theology is a more useful resource for clarification of their complex 'new' theories that they imagined.[5]

By interweaving chapters dealing with one debate then the other, I provide the reader (who must promise to be patient with unfamiliar language and perhaps abhorrent beliefs) with an experience of imaginative cross-pollination that I hope may bear fruit. This provision is limited to the field of metaphysics as it is the basis of both assertions (although repudiated in one). As such, I do not pretend to offer a comprehensive theology of the Eucharist or a sociological analysis of transgender; although points from both disciplines are mentioned to contextualise my explanations in language that may be more familiar to the reader, I am not attempting to settle ongoing arguments in either although I do hope that this book may enable more fruitful debate.

For readers interested in a wider context for each debate, I wholeheartedly recommend Pat (now Patrick) Califia's *Sex Changes: The Politics of Transgenderism* (now *Sex Changes: Transgender Politics*) and *The Eucharist* by Edward Schillebeeckx, O.P.

---

[4] The same could be said about their ignorance of performance values – which less time tapping at the computer and more time treading the boards may have solved.

[5] See Eco/1984; Broadie/1995.

First published in 1997 and 1968, respectively, the former (since updated) is balanced, critical and compassionate; the latter is erudite, ecumenical and concise. Both provide an informed, detailed and referenced historical context for the present debates.

As this creation has occasioned much quotation, I take the usual responsibility for my errors and issue the usual disclaimers for my juxtaposition of texts which may not have been written with the intention or the meaning I discover in them. In other words, while I am very grateful for all the help I have been given to write this book, don't blame anyone else for the content!

Please also don't give up when my initially light-hearted style turns more heavy-going. This book is not only written for theologians and critical theorists but for everyone for whom the questions raised by either transubstantiation or transgender are personal issues more felt with the heart than reasoned with the head. Footnotes and references are there for those who wish to investigate further but I hope that the flow of the developing argument is clear enough that any unfamiliar vocabulary necessary to understanding it can be learned along the way. Please do read the chapters that appear to be dedicated to 'the other debate' (than the one you are most interested in) as the argument for both debates is developed, often explicitly, even in a footnote, in all chapters. So if you don't read them, you'll miss out!

I am also writing for people who hold totally opposing views in each debate. So that's four sets of people who may at times be tempted to chuck this book across the room and start screaming in rage! If I appear at times to be pandering to one then the other, it may be that (as well as working out my own developing argument) I am acknowledging that each may be partly right. However, points which I initially support may prove later to be untenable in the light of other arguments – so do bear with me if you can possibly stand it. The mellifluous words of Seneca (on little boys among books as bees among flowers) may be applied to writers:

> they gather nectar not their own but, by dint of their labour of appropriation and transformation, theirs is the honey of that harvest.[6]

Our discussion starts with a traditional folksong, with actions, which is not in origin as peaceful as the scene described by Seneca.

---

[6] My paraphrase of Bill Marsh's quote of Michel de Montaigne plagiarising Seneca, in *Plagiarism: Alchemy and Remedy in Higher Education*: Marsh/2007/82.

1 – Disputes over presence & change

Catholic leaders say Hokey Cokey is 'faith hate'
(*The Scotsman*, 22 December 2008)

It's safe to say that many people reading this headline would be tempted to turn the page. What's wrong with football fans singing a folksong to mock their rivals? Although I am a member of the Scottish Roman Catholic community, I confess that when I taught Religious, Moral & Philosophical Studies I would have been filled with delight if any of my pupils (fooball fans or not) knew that the hokey-cokey 'was composed by Puritans during the 18th century in an attempt to mock the actions and language of priests leading Latin mass' (*ibid*).

Folksongs and children's games often innocently echo horrible events in history: the Black Death, the Great Fire of London, the beheading of Mary Queen of Scots – all these grisly stories transformed into circle dances, choral rounds and skipping games come from the same folk memory as the hokey-cokey.

So I don't disagree with the spokesman for the RC Church in Scotland:

> This song does have quite disturbing origins. It was devised as an attack on, and a parody of, the Catholic mass. (*ibid*)[7]

This same newspaper article points out that both 'hokey-cokey' and 'hocus pocus' are terms of contempt – being corruptions of '*hoc est corpus meum*' ('this is my body') which are the words of 'consecration' (or 'institution' in

---

[7] Peter Kearney, spokesman for Cardinal O'Brien (then leader of the Catholic Church in Scotland).

Protestant theology) used during the Latin mass.[8] In other words, these terms try to equate the metaphysics of transubstantiation with magic: 'priestcraft' = witchcraft.

Transubstantiation, which is what all the fuss is about, means the transformation of a (necessary) essence, while the 'accidents' (unnecessary characteristics of something) are unchanged. For example, in the case of the Scottish Saltire flag, the diagonal cross of St Andrew would be 'necessary' for all flags which are the Scottish Saltire whereas the size and material of any *particular* flag would be 'accidental'.

So it looks like bread, it tastes like bread but it's *really* the body of Christ. Even apart from the strain of suspending our judgement of the evidence of our senses, this language just sounds so mediaeval! Talk of metaphysical essences and accidents nowadays can cause us to smile. But we may understand this language better if we think of the common experience of mistaking someone for someone else: they *look* the same, but they're not *really*. 'Identical' twins often have fun with this but would be most miffed if it were suggested that they were really the same person!

Christianity has always been concerned to express clearly what is real. The problem of reality versus appearances was the major concern of Plato and the reason why the language of transubstantiation may strike us as mediaeval is because scholars during that period (especially 'scholastic theologians' – or 'schoolmen') used the work of Plato, or his most famous pupil Aristotle, to try to express clearly what they believed about Holy Communion.

---

[8] These words come from the Latin 'Vulgate' translation of the Gospel accounts. See Fillion/1887.

It's sometimes forgotten that theologians, Catholic or Protestant,[9] are not necessarily committed to either Platonic language to express what they believe about God, nor to Aristotelian language to express what they believe about the Eucharist. 'Eucharist', from the Greek for 'thanksgiving', is the word Catholics tend to use for Holy Communion. I say 'Catholics' rather than 'Roman Catholics' as Anglican and Episcopalian churches have members who hold Catholic views as well as those who hold Protestant views.[10]

There is a famous painting in the Vatican called *The School of Athens* which shows, in the centre, Plato pointing up (to indicate eternal truth) and Aristotle pointing down (indicating changing appearances).

If we think of their philosophical – or rather metaphysical – concepts as frameworks upon which words have been woven in an attempt to picture clearly complex beliefs, then I will argue that the vertical and horizontal alignment of these frameworks not only support but also *constrain* any tapestry of words woven on them. Eucharistic theologians have twisted and strained their language in their attempt to express their multifaceted faith, yet all their shades of meaning can be reduced – by those impatient with theological nuances – to black and white. And that leads to divisive newspaper headlines.

---

[9] As the main bone of contention over the Eucharist is between these two groups, I limit my discussion by omitting an analysis of the Orthodox position. (The main dogmatic contention between the Roman Catholic and Orthodox Church is the creedal *filioque*).

[10] I also respect the usage of Christians such as the Revd John Bell of the Iona Community, who while proud of their Protestant heritage claim the word Catholic because they belong to the universal church. 'Catholic' comes from the Greek word *katholiki* meaning 'universal'.

Add to this division an anxiety about the unique nature of truth — which I believe comes from the Inquisition; an obsession with *absolute* truths and a compulsion to ban, battle and burn those who imagine other metaphysical alignments and a wider spectrum of conceptual colour and we have reasons why all during the history of the Christian church, and still today, non-Christian observers have said with glee or despair, parodying the words of St. Paul in Acts, 'see how these Christians hate one another'.

Antipathy in disagreement is, of course, not unknown outside the chapel and the cloister — and even the hallowed halls of Academia can witness displays of professional pique, as the next chapter illustrates.

2 – The trouble with gender

> If you ask experts at medical centres how often a child is born so noticeably atypical in terms of genitalia that a specialist in sex differentiation is called in, the number comes out to about 1 in 1500 to 1 in 2000 births. But a lot more people than that are born with subtler forms of sex anatomy variations, some of which won't show up until later in life.
> (Intersex Society of North America)[11]

My mother, who both delivered and assisted at the delivery of many babies over the decades when she worked as a State Registered Nurse and Midwife, was surprised when I asked her if there had ever been any doubt as to the sex of the baby. In all her years she'd not only never witnessed this but had never heard of such a situation. So, although no-one could dispute that very rare cases of physiological intersexuality do occur, I am wary of using the (mostly female) midwife-blaming language that suggests a series of ambiguously sexed babies coming down a factory conveyor belt and being *arbitrarily* assigned a sex. I don't feel it's unreasonable, especially if we accept the language in the statement about gender, 'Alan identifies [himself] as a man', to accept a statement about sex, 'the midwife identified the baby as male'.

Although interrelated, the categorical difference between physiology and ideology is clear in these statements by Georgiann Davis (2015/113): 'Intersex people are born with bodies that directly challenge the sex binary'; and Judith Butler (1999/12): 'sex could not qualify as a prediscursive anatomical facticity'.

---

[11] www.isna.org/faq/frequency accessed 1st April 2017

While the starting point for Davis[12] is that there are people whose bodies do not fit into medical categories of sex (which therefore need to be reconsidered),[13] Butler builds her critique of gender on complex theoretical foundations. I am not a medical doctor and have nothing to say about physiology (apart from the observation that bodies feel extremely factual and to dismiss them as theoretical constructions appears to be, at least, a little unfeeling). As a metaphysician, I have a lot to say about theory – especially when it strays into the area of 'the nature of nature'.

The conflation of the terms 'sex' and 'gender' is where all the trouble begins. In tracing a history of ideas, it really helps if writers admit whom they are plagiarising. It's especially nice if they actually provide clear references so we know who said what, who said it first and who thought it first. In theory. In practice, that old adage from the Bible, already old when it was recorded, still rings true: 'there is nothing new under the sun' (Ecclesiastes 1:9).

So, while Butler helpfully provides extensive references and transparently depends upon (and argues with) French post-structuralism and feminism, Michel Foucault is less transparent when it comes to admitting the similarity of his main strategy of reading against the grain with that of the North African Jacques Derrida, and that of his variously-named theories of political subjectivity with those of the RC radical educator Ivan Illich in South America.

---

[12] Whose book, *Contesting Intersex: The Dubious Diagnosis*, I wholeheartedly recommend.

[13] See Paula Gaudenzi & Francisco Ortega for an evaluation of the critical work of Michel Foucault and Ivan Illich as resources for demedicalization (Gaudenzi & Ortega/2012). The article is in Portuguese but one abstract and many references are in English.

Despite protestations from the overwhelming number of avowed materialists in academia, it can be helpful to keep the formative religious influences on critical theorists in mind. I say this because, otherwise, we may miss the relevance of the statement that the history of gender starts with grammatical difference.

Even the intransigent antitransgenderist Sheila Jeffreys does not disagree with this start to the story – however much she does with the subsequent use of the term:

> The term 'gender' itself is problematic. It was first used in a sense that was not simply about grammar by sexologists – the scientists of sex such as John Money in the 1950s and 1960s – who were involved in normalising intersex infants. They used the term to mean the behavioural characteristics they considered most appropriate for persons of one or other biological sex [...] Their purpose was not progressive. (Jeffreys/2014/4)

As grammatical 'gender' was appropriated by sexologists, linguistic 'grammatology' was appropriated by the father of deconstruction, Jacques Derrida, born in the then French territory of Algeria (to an Arabic-speaking Jewish family), who in 1967 published his famous book of that name. Though Derrida and Foucault (brought up in a strict mainland French Roman Catholic family) had a long-lasting argument over metaphysics, even the titles of two of their most famous books (*Of Grammatology*; *Words and Things*) evidence their focus on the significance of the word for their theoretical enterprise. The modern belief in words as constitutive of reality is rooted in the Biblical understanding: *In principio erat Verbum* (John 1:1).

Unsurprisingly, Judith Butler gives precedence to the influence of various female authors on her work of critical theory. As well as the theoretical and experiential heritage of feminists such as Simone de Beauvoir, Monique Wittig and Luce Irigaray, she also references the anthropological research of Margaret Mead – whose reflections on her sojourn on Samoa have produced very different responses. Shira Tarrant, in *When Sex Became Gender*, sees her work as ground-breaking in terms of the social construction of gender, referencing:

> Margaret Mead's cross-cultural comparisons of sex-role ideology, of reciprocal and reinforcing influences between sociopolitical structures, and of social constructions of womanhood. (Tarrant/2006/8)

Geoffrey Samson, in *Educating Eve*, sees Mead's work as fraudulent:

> Her reputation derives from a description of the society of Samoa, based on nine months' stay in her early twenties, with no previous knowledge of the Samoan language, as a guest of a white family resident on a Samoan island. The description has turned out to be not just over-romanticized, but a preposterous travesty of the truth about Samoan life. (Samson/1997/105)[14]

---

[14] Samson (op. cit./173, n.105) provides references for both views: 'Mead on Samoa: *Margaret Mead, Coming of Age in Samoa: A Psychological Study of Primitive Youth for Western Civilization*, W. Morrow (New York), 1928; Mead's account a travesty: D. Freeman, *Margaret Mead and Samoa*, Harvard University Press, 1983.'

Whatever the lasting value of Mead's 'popular trade book about adolescence',[15] on publication it challenged both the popular and the academic assumption that early 20th century White middle class American sexual *mores* were not only normal but universal. Mead's primitivist assumptions would be challenged in *Triste Tropiques* (1995) by Claude Lévi-Strauss but it is his structuralist pairing of sex/ gender and nature/ culture that Butler takes issue with:

> If Lévi-Strauss's framework were true, it would be possible to trace the transformation of sex into gender, by locating that stable mechanism of cultures, the exchange rules of kinship, which effect that transformation in fairly regular ways. (Butler/1999/47)

Butler's rebuttal makes use of language often encountered in works of critical theorists, and rarely explained, the language of signification:

> The binary relation between culture and nature promotes a relationship of hierarchy in which culture freely "imposes" meaning on nature, and, hence, renders it into an "Other" to be appropriated to its own limitless uses, safeguarding the ideality of the signifier and the structure of signification on the model of domination. (Butler/1999/48)

---

[15] As Paul Shankman (2009/112) describes it. In contrast, he describes her subsequent monograph, *Social Organization of Manu'a*, as 'sober and scholarly, building on earlier descriptions of the islands' *(ibid)*.

The topic of signs and signification is of great importance to Christians in their fractious dialogue over the Eucharist, as the next chapter shows.

3 – Lord, unite us in this sign

The controversy over the significance of Communion continues to divide Christian denominations. This controversy involves deeply held values, which is unsurprising as it is over the very body and blood of Jesus Christ. I recall even two good friends and flatmates, in a sunny university Chaplaincy garden in St. Andrews, in heated discussion over the use for Communion of 'crumbly bread'.

The discussion did not centre on leavened versus unleavened bread but on the crumbs. Nicky's Catholic piety was outraged by Sharon's statement: 'If there's any leftover we feed it to the birds', and Sharon's Methodist sensibilities outraged in turn when Nicky countered with the need to consume, respectfully bury or reserve the fragments.

The disposal of crumbs after Communion may seem peripheral to the historically developing subtle metaphysics of the Eucharistic argument; but as well as causing religious outrage it is also an acid test of theological stance.

This religious outrage is unfortunately not limited to fractious flatmates sitting in sunny varsity gardens. I am not saying that the main reason why followers of two famous Glasgow football teams beat each other up is metaphysical – but any division that causes religious factions to deeply devalue each other should be overcome. Fortunately, not all representatives of the divided denominations of Christianity are as violent in their disagreement as some football supporters. There is a long history of attempts to find a solution to the Eucharistic controversy, continuing to the present day.

When the Anglican and Roman Catholic International Commission reported in 1988 'substantial agreement' on their Eucharistic theology, the Lambeth Conference of the same year responded positively:

> This Conference:
> Recognises the Agreed Statements of ARCIC I on 'Eucharistic Doctrine, Ministry and Ordination,' and their Elucidations, as consonant in substance with the faith of Anglicans and believes that this agreement offers a sufficient basis for taking the next step forward towards the reconciliation of our Churches grounded in agreement in faith.[16]

However, some Roman Catholics (and Anglicans) felt the language of the ARCIC 'Agreed Statements', Vatican 'Observations' and ARCIC 'Elucidations' was open to ambiguous interpretation, as a later statement (from the United States Conference of Catholic Bishops) shows:

> The use of phrases such as *substantial agreement*, *substantial identity* and *consonant in substance* in The Final Report and in the Vatican response to it has been widely criticized as ambiguous. *Substantial* and *in substance* can mean either 'in very large part' or 'fundamental, basic'. In addition, the term *substantial* carries overtones from various historical theological

---

[16] 'Resolution 8' from the Lambeth Conference of 1988, 'Anglican-Roman Catholic International Commission (ARCIC)' www.lambethconference.org/resolutions/1988/1988-8.cfm Paragraph 1, accessed 12/04/08.

controversies and from its use in scholastic theology.[17]

The members of the commission, after their heart-searching attempts to find theological common ground may have felt disgruntled at such a scholastic response; however it highlights the bone of contention to be not so much theological as metaphysical.[18] In other words, for traditional Roman Catholics it is important that Eucharistic change and presence is not just spiritual but also physical; that, despite appearances, when Christ said, 'This is my body' (Matt. 40:26; Mark 14:22; Luke 22:19) he meant exactly that.

However the problem for traditional Christians is not about the miracles and meaning of bread in the ministry of the historical Jesus of Nazareth, nor even principally about the various Gospel narratives of the Upper Room. The problem rather is about their commemoration of that narrative, and the miracle or meaning they acknowledge in their Eucharistic liturgy today. Among these problems is the cultural diversity of views on the power of memory, and of the word, to make present a past event.

---

[17] 'How Can We Recognize 'Substantial Agreement'?'
'Anglican-Roman Catholic Consultation-USA, April 5, 1993'
'United States Conference of Catholic Bishops', paragraph 19
http://www.usccb.org/seia/arc_substantialagreement_1993.shtml
accessed 11/04/08. 'The Final Report', published in 1981, finalised
the deliberations of ARCIC I; ARCIC II spanned 1983-2005;
ARCIC III, begun in 2016, is on-going. Currently information on
Anglican-Roman Catholic dialogue is available at
https://iarccum.org
[18] Indeed the document ARCCM-16 is a deliberation by J.R. Lucas,
Fellow of Merton College, Oxford, on the metaphysical, or
substantial, *vinculum* (invisible cement joining 'monads', basically)
of Gottfried Wilhelm Leibniz https://iarccum.org/archives/arccm

In those narratives, the Greek 'words of consecration' as Catholics call them; or 'words of institution' as Protestants prefer, are:

τουτό εστι το σωμά μου
(Mark/ Κατα Μαρκον 14:40)[19]

Joachim Jeremias responds to the claim that the indicative pronoun 'this' refers not to a noun but an action:

It was not the action of breaking the bread or of pouring out the wine that Jesus interpreted, but rather the bread and the wine itself. This is supported by two observations: first that the interpretation of the special elements in the Jewish Passover rite, which was the precedent for the form of Jesus' words of interpretation, is not concerned with any actions, but with the components of the meal themselves; and secondly, that the whole Early Church has from the beginning understood the τουτο as referring to the bread and wine (Cf. I Cor. 11.25 τουτο = τουτο το ποτηριον). (Jeremias/1966/221)

This theological and philosophical preoccupation with the objects that words refer to, and how secure that reference is, has spilled over into critical theory following the famous lectures of Ferdinand de Saussure. The elaboration of linguistic theory on signs following their publication is the subject of the next chapter.

---

[19] All the synoptic Gospels have the same words. All Greek quotation of scripture from *Novvm Testamentvm Graece* (Souter/1941).

4 – Signs

If the sequence of chapters have appeared, so far, to be more in parallel than interwoven, then this chapter is where a considerable crossover occurs. In my introduction, I observed that the scorn of many (not all) modern critical theorists for the debates of mediaeval scholastics and classical philosophers gives the impression to readers that all their postmodern and post-structuralist ideas are new. In the case of the debate over signs and signification, nothing could be further from the truth.

In this debate, it is unfortunate that the body of work which has come down to us in the name of Ferdinand de Saussure was not actually written by him but was compiled by Albert Sechehaye and Charles Bally, from their notes on his famous lectures at the University of Geneva in a period of five years just prior to the First World War.

Cours de linguistique générale (1916) is, of course, written in French so monoglot English speakers have the added filter of translation of a text already composed by two different writers from their interpretation of their notes handwritten in a crowded lecture hall – when abstract theories of communication were perhaps the last thing on a young man's mind.

The resulting text, and the reader's reaction to it, would not be any problem at all for many critical theorists such as Derrida whose famous cry of *il n'y a pas de hors-texte* (itself subject to a variety of translation) may be understood as an affirmation of the dialogical nature of writing – that the meaning of a text is never final and that nothing is outside of the text; not that nothing exists outside of it, but rather that the text itself is only understandable in the context supplied by the event of reading it.

So, in some ways, it doesn't matter what those young Swiss men sitting in Saussure's lecture hall made of his *Cours de linguistique générale*; what is important now is what the book (in French or in translation) means to us in our situation today. In Biblical Studies, the former concern is called 'heuristics', and the latter 'hermeneutics' – both terms are widely used by critical theorists (although their distinction is not always clear).

This unfolding story of the thinking, speaking, listening, writing and reading of a book (with much annotation, abbreviation, clarification, omission, addition, mis/translation, and other editing processes also going on) is a useful example of what Saussure (may have) meant by 'the detachment of the signified from the signifier'.

In other words, does the name (or 'signifier') 'Ferdinand de Saussure', as understood ('signified') today have anything at all do with one Ferdinand de Saussure, the eminent Swiss academic who gave a series of lectures comprising a course on General Linguistics at the University of Geneva from 1906-1911? Even the above paragraph already runs into difficulties, in exploring Ferdinand de Saussure's (which one?) concept of a 'sign' composed of 'signifier' and 'signified'.

Umberto Eco playfully (and murderously) referred to this problem when he named his first novel, *Il nome della Rosa* (The Name of the Rose) – as '*rosa nulla est*' (the rose is not) is a famous Latin philosophical and philological conundrum. A variation on this is the English line 'a rose by any other name would smell as sweet' from Shakespeare's *Romeo and Juliet* – where Juliet argues that Romeo's name is accidental to his nature. He is her sweet lover, it does not matter that his name happens to be Romeo Montague (which signifies that his family is the enemy of hers) as it could be any name at all. Eco's reference takes this problem further: can it be true that names are not only arbitrary but that they are so arbitrary that something can be named that does not even exist?

If we substitute the word 'name' for 'sign' or 'pronoun' or 'identity', we can see how relevant this seemingly playful and abstract argument is to the gender trouble occurring today (which some maintain has always occurred but the difference is that today we take it seriously).

Mediaeval scholastics, the critical theorists of their day, were well-versed in this argument, which they named 'nominalism' vs 'antinominalism'. The words 'nominal' (in name only) and 'nominate' (to name) surviving in English provide a translation.

Alexander Broadie (1990/8) provides an example: cat A and cat B are both cats – but how do we know this, in what does their common cathood consist and where does it reside? (No, please don't bang your head off the nearest brick wall, philosophers will go on like this and usually about tables; so thinking about cats is a lot more fun. And it should help us think more clearly about the topics of this book. Honest.)

The nominalist answer is that cathood is just a family resemblance, among all things cattish, that we happen to notice and it's no more than a mental category. In other words we just made it up. Simple!

Hmmm. As a thought experiment, stop reading for a moment while you make a mental list (or better still ask someone else to, while you write it down) of what makes a cat a cat. I asked my mother and her answers are over the page. *Stop! Get your own!*

At first my mother answered the question quite literally, with, 'DNA, evolution, parentage'. Then I asked her what makes a cat a cat rather than some other kind of animal; she said, 'it's not a dog'. Then I asked her, if she saw something without her glasses and only as she came near recognised it as a cat, what characteristics of a cat she would recognise. She said 'it's small but it's not a fox, and a cat has whiskers but it's not a hare or a rabbit; it walks stealthily and it meows'.

We could separate these cat-egories (*sorry!*) into biochemical, microbiological, genetic, chromosomal, genealogical, biological, visual, auditory, taxonomic, adjectival, phenomenological, adverbial, physiological and behavioural, etc. – with much overlap and many more debates over where one category ends and another begins as well as how many categories we would need to exhaustively identify the phenomenon commonly signified by the signifier 'a cat'.

Saussure spoke (or at least was quoted as speaking) of diachronic and synchronic signs, meaning in this case that the sign 'a cat' has changed in meaning over time (as have cats) and that as well as identifying the location of a sign on its timeline, we can also specify it more clearly by noting its difference from other, adjacent, signs.[20]

So my mother's answers, those of a nonagenarian lady asked without preparation and given off-the-cuff, may also be categorised in these terms: DNA, evolution and parentage all refer to diachronic development of the sign; the others refer to the discrete, synchronic, location of the

---

[20] I am not defending any particular theory of taxonomy here; there is some similarity between Saussure's categories and Wittgenstein's identification of 'family resemblance' or (a more recent development) 'cluster concept'.

sign in the semantic field of reference: 'a cat' is not 'a dog' nor 'a fox', nor 'a hare' nor 'a rabbit' – all being things that one might see from a distance (or without glasses) and mistake for a cat. Especially in my mother's garden or nearby fields.

Let's leave the question of how one sign can qualify another (e.g. 'a cat' and 'has whiskers') for just now and simply observe that 'has whiskers', 'is small', 'walks stealthily' and 'meows' each mark off the sign 'a cat' from others that lack these characteristics.

If you're already shaking your head and thinking of cats of your acquaintance that are not small, don't have whiskers, don't walk stealthily or don't meow, then I thank you for bringing up the problem of universals and particulars.

The antinominalist (or 'realist') answer is that cathood is an objective universal reality irrespective of any particular local manifestations – such as a cat with only one ear, etc. Some mediaeval philosophers would say that this reality exists in the Mind of God. This idea may therefore be called mentalism – although it is also called idealism, realism (and even materialism)[21] such is the capacity for categorical confusion in later ages, notably today. The confusion mostly arises when the Mind of God is confused with either human imagination, or with the mind of any individual philosopher – a claim of unscientific *hubris*.[22]

This variously named idea appeals to an objective reality existing independently of subjective viewpoints, a reality often considered to be (only) mathematically or

[21] I discuss this point in Chapter 6.
[22] This difference is not only one of faith but of epistemology – the science of knowledge. No human perspective (or mindset) can pretend to absolute objectivity.

scientifically comprehensible. So my mother's initial answers, DNA, evolution and parentage, could be considered as antinominalist: *i.e.* chromosomes don't change according to how you feel about them.

Or do they? There were four other categories that, in our discussion, my mother decided (mostly because I questioned them) were unfitting to the question: 'What makes a cat a cat?' These were: environment, treatment, conditions, weather. All four of these categories certainly affect how a cat appears (or disappears) so do they all affect how a cat *is*?

The relationship between appearance and reality is not only crucial in the debate over transgender but central to the debate over transubstantiation, and the next chapter introduces the views of various reformers.

5 – Transubstantiation: that's what it's all about!

The historical controversy over Communion which continues to divide Christian denominations involves deeply held values, which is unsurprising as it is over the very body and blood of Jesus Christ. Martin Luther and the Swiss radical reformer Ulrich Zwingli differed considerably in their theological stance over the presence of Christ in the Eucharist. In his biography of Zwingli, Jean Rilliet quotes their heated correspondence of 1526. Luther stated:

> 'The mouth carnally eats the Body of Christ...but the heart seizes the word through the apprehension of faith and eats it spiritually.' (Rilliet/1964/232)

Zwingli disagreed: 'He dwells in our hearts by faith, and not by corporeal eating through our mouths.' (*op. cit.*/232). The Marburg Colloquy of 1529 brought no solution. Collated accounts of four witnesses record Luther, whose position has been termed 'consubstantation', chalking on the table *hoc est corpus meum* (this is my body) and Zwingli in tears at his intransigence (*op. cit.*/256,262,264). The Roman Catholic position seems similarly intransigent to many Christians, across the whole spectrum of the Reformed Church. The *Catechism of the Catholic Church*, prepared following the Second Vatican Ecumenical Council of 1962-1965, in Article 3 paragraph 1400, states:

> Ecclesial communities derived from the Reformation and separated from the Catholic Church 'have not preserved the proper reality of the Eucharistic mystery in its fullness, especially because of the absence of the sacrament of Holy Orders.' It is for this reason that Eucharistic

intercommunion with these communities is not possible with the Catholic Church. (Ratzinger *et al.*/1995/316)[23]

The struggle of theologians past and present to find creative concepts and fitting language in which to express their Eucharistic doctrine can be summarised, very broadly, as a division over whether the body and blood of Christ is present subjectively or objectively in the Eucharist. In other terms, a division over value versus substance; a bone of contention not so much theological as metaphysical.

Even so, Raymond Moloney SJ notes the theological tension between the Roman Catholic followers of the schools of Thomas Aquinas and Duns Scotus:

> Thomists follow St Thomas in presenting the doctrine of Eucharistic Change as the meaning of scripture. Scotists […] accept it as a requirement of church teaching […] Left to themselves, they would have preferred the position which came to be known as consubstatiation, according to which the bread and wine after the consecration remain in their natural substances but coexist with the body and blood of Christ. (Moloney/ 1995/146)

So recourse to the Greek doesn't help us. It has been rightly asserted that Jesus would not have spoken Greek but rather the homespun dialect of Syro-Aramaic to his Galilean followers, or even, in keeping with the solemnity

---

[23] The Catechism quotes the Vatican II document (21st Nov. 1964) *Unitatis redintegratio* 22, 3. Cardinal Ratzinger, soon to become Pope Benedict XVI, chaired the Commission which produced the draft document.

of Passovertide, Hebrew. The verb 'to be' has no equivalent term in Hebrew or in Aramaic, its meaning is derived from context. Joseph Stallings, author of *Rediscovering Passover*, comments on both the verbal and the phrasal meaning understood in Aramaic and Hebrew:

> Great care must be taken in any discussion of the Greek verb *'estin'* not to ignore the fact that the original Aramaic *'Den Bisri'* can only mean 'This is my body'. The Greek translation can say no less than that and be honest. [...] The Hebrew idiom *basar-dam* or the Aramaic *bisra-adam*, both of which mean 'flesh and blood', was the Semitic idiomatic phrase meaning 'a person'. The disciples understood that [in] Jesus' words of institution [...] *he was giving each and every one of them his whole and entire self!* (Stallings/c.1988/218 & 216, emphasis original)

Roman Catholics, Lutherans, Calvinists and Zwinglians accept that, despite appearances to the contrary, Christians encounter Christ's 'whole and entire self' really present in the Eucharist; but they differ on the explanation. These four Eucharistic theologies are often described, respectively, as: transubstantiation; consubstantiation; participation and memorial. However this is to gloss over the historical and continuing work of theologians from these denominations, developing their Eucharistic theology in accordance with, or in counterpoint to, each other's understanding.

There is also the debate about who is empowered to effect the transubstantiation (and to proclaim that it has taken place). Fritz Kemmler highlights this polemic in a Mystery Play (one of a traditional Mediaeval Cycle from which the modern, more familiar, school and parish Nativity Play derives):

> I am the verey bread of liffe.
> From heaven I light and am send.
> Whoe eateth that bread, man or wiffe,
> Shall lyve with me withowt end.
> And that bread that I you give,
> Your wicked life to amend,
> *Becomes* my fleshe through your *beleeffe*
> And doth release your sinful band.
> (Chester Mystery Cycle, 'The Resurrection')[24]

Kemmler notes that this ambiguous wording may be interpreted to underline the agency of the recipient (singular or plural) rather than that of the priest who administers the sacrament, and concludes:

> It appears that some of the views on the Sacrament of the Eucharist propagated and entertained by Wyclif and his adherents have influenced this new presentation of "transubstantiation" in play 18 of *The Chester Mystery Cycle*. (Kemmler/1998/212)

Wyclif, as an early English herald of the Reformation, was famously concerned more with the *Ecclesia*, the church (the Body of Christ) as gathered congregation, rather than the *Magisterium*, its ruling head. He was also keen on vernacular (English) translation of the scriptures – and was burned at the stake for his beliefs. The view expressed above, which came to be known as 'the priesthood of all believers', was deemed heretical yet it survives in the still-quoted Roman Catholic maxim

---

[24] Play 18, 170-177, emphasis Kemmler (Kemmler/1998/211).

Ecclesia supplet ('the Church supplies') used to remedy defective performance of sacramental ritual by the presiding priest.[25]

Different as these theological positions are, they are all working within a common Platonic metaphysical paradigm; or within its development by his pupil, Aristotle. Kilian McDonnel OSB points out that Calvin 'adhered to the formulations of Chalcedon' and that his 'Christological dialectic is clearly stated within a Platonic framework' (both quotes McDonnell 1967/214).

However Christianity is not necessarily committed to either a Platonic framework for its creed nor an Aristotelian framework to express its Eucharistic theology. Focusing on the reality of the Eucharistic mystery which the Roman Catholic Church (under one metaphysical paradigm) has called transubstantiation, I argue that an eirenic solution may be provided by a present day 'pagan philosopher' Robert M. Pirsig whose metaphysics of Quality,[26] in which 'substance' is composed by 'a static pattern of values', can express this mysterious reality in its

---

[25] For example if a priest forgets to speak certain ritual words, but all other elements, including his intention, are present and correct, the Church supplies the necessary validation of the transformation. The question of the disposition of agency is also one for the debate over transgender, where the surgeon may assume the official role of the priest, validly ordained to carry out this ritual transformation – and various social groupings (partner, peers, friends, family, colleagues, passersby, social media contacts) assume the role of the gathered community. For such transformation to take place, does it need to be validated by a wider social grouping than that of the authority (singular or plural) presiding at the altar or in the operating theatre?

[26] Pirsig capitalises (Dynamic) Quality to differentiate it from static quality. The difference is explained in detail in subsequent chapters.

fullness to the satisfaction of both Reformed and Catholic theology, and remove at least this bar to intercommunion.

'Substance' is obviously a key word in both debates; the next chapter explores this mediaeval metaphysical concept still in use today.

6 – A matter of substance

Judith Butler sees the concept of substance to be a major contributor to the view that a binary category of sex is essential to the being of a person:

> What is the metaphysics of substance and how does it inform thinking about the categories of sex? In the first instance, humanist conceptions of the subject tend to assume a substantive person who is the bearer of various essential and nonessential attributes. (Butler/1999/14)

In Alexander Broadie's example of a cat, we recall the antinominalist (or realist) view which assumes exactly that: a cat is defined as a being who is the bearer of the essential attributes of cathood; a particular moggie may have only one ear, a wet coat or a nasty temper, but these attributes are nonessential or accidental. The important thing is that a cat of substance possesses cathood. Note that we don't need to decide which attributes are essential in order for this theory to appear coherent – and it rapidly becomes incoherent when we try to. Butler takes a nominalist view (although she doesn't say this):

> The universal conception of the person, however, is displaced as a point of departure for a social theory of gender by those historical and anthropological positions that understand gender as a relation among socially constituted subjects in specifiable contexts. This relational or contextual point of view suggests that what the person "is", and, indeed, what gender "is", is always relative to the constructed relations in which it is determined. (Butler/1999/14-15)

What is interesting here is that Butler is *not* claiming that, individually, any one of us can be successful in a speech-act of social self-determination – but rather that determination of identity (not only of gender) is socially, specifically, locally and temporarily constructed. So she is parting company with antinominalists – who still comprise a surprisingly large company and include most 'hard' scientists.[27]

The lines of demarcation between metaphysical views shift and blur as each side attempts to solve the conceptual problems created by the other side's latest attempt to solve theirs. So from the view that 'a cat' is a sign always and everywhere recognised, the opposite contention (that it's just an arbitrary and conventional way to speak about a group of similar-seeming animals) gives rise to another possible view: that the conceptual content of 'a cat' is influenced by our experience.

A thumbnail description of major metaphysical views of 'a cat' could therefore be: a universal Idea, forgotten at birth but clearly recognised when encountered (Plato); the substance of formed matter that bears the accidental attributes of a particular cat (Aristotle); an unstable collection of sense data such as tabby stripes, meows, a feeling of fur, feline odours (David Hume); a previous (*a priori*) idea that develops with experience of particular cats (Immanuel Kant).

Before moving on to consider the modern metaphysical view that I feel would be most helpful to critical theorists of gender like Butler, and to Christians trying to worship

---

[27] Including Richard Dawkins: 'You and I, we humans, we animals, inhabit a virtual world, constructed from elements that are, at successively higher levels, useful for representing the real world.' (Dawkins/1998/275). See McManus/2011/254,185-186.

together, I want us to note that her assertion of social construction is not only for concepts of gender but also for identity and (it could be argued) for existence itself.

Theoretical abstraction can seem very tedious indeed and critical theory is rarely an exception (especially when the lyricism of lucid French speculation is translated into the turgid prose of Anglo-Saxon pedantry). Why should we care what a blasted cat is, metaphysically? What's at stake? Nothing less than the lives of the millions of human beings currently oppressed under the sign of 'women', as sex is associated with reproduction, exploited through gender as labour. Returning to Butler on Levi-Strauss:

> Within such a view, "sex" is [...] culturally and politically undetermined, providing the "raw material" of culture [...] that begins to signify only through and after its subjection to kinship.
>
> This very concept of sex-as-matter, sex-as-instrument-of-cultural-signification, however, is a discursive formation that acts as a naturalized foundation for the nature/culture distinction and the strategies of domination that that distinction supports. (Butler/1999/47-48)

Aristotle's view of *matter* was that it has no other characteristics apart from quantity (normally named 'extension' by philosophers, such as Descartes) whereas the *substance* of a cat or a human has only those attributes which are essential – *i.e.* those common to all cats or humans. It is the *accidents* which make a particular cat.

What Butler is protesting about is the structuralist pairing of nature/ culture and female/ woman: *i.e.* female is to woman as nature is to culture – something to serve as raw material and be dominated. The raw and the cooked.

7 – Scripture narratives

Judith Butler, and feminists in general, are not alone in wanting to reverse value systems they consider abhorrent. I find it a striking common feature of the Gospel narratives of Mark 14:3-9, Matthew 26:6-13, Luke 22:24-27, John 12:1-11 & 13:3-7 that in all these passages (either part of, or proximate to, the narrative of the Eucharistic meal in the Upper Room) the male disciples appear to desire to be benefactors and in control. Jesus upsets this desire and disturbs their sense of seemliness: by letting a woman anoint his head or his feet with an expensive ointment, by charging them to act as servants, and by modelling service in washing their feet. Their values are not his values. Jesus prophesies of the woman (who has braved leprosy and men's anger in order to make her valuable libation) that what she has done will be told in memory of her. Soon he will tell the disciples that they too must break and pour out what he gives at great cost.

> Jesus was at Bethany in the house of Simon the leper, he was at dinner when a woman came in with an alabaster jar of very costly ointment, pure nard. She broke the jar and poured the ointment on his head. Some who were there said to one another indignantly, 'Why this waste of ointment?' 'Ointment like this could have been sold for over 300 denarii and the money given to the poor'; and they were angry with her. But Jesus said, 'Leave her alone. Why are you upsetting her? What she has done for me is one of the good works. You have the poor with you always, and you can be kind to them whenever you wish, but you will not always have me. She

35

has done what was in her power to do: she has anointed my body beforehand for its burial. I tell you solemnly, whenever throughout all the world the Good News is proclaimed, what she has done will be told also, in remembrance of her. (Mark 14:3-9)[28]

In the similar passage in Matthew 26:6-13 it is the disciples who complain and in John 12:1-11 it is Judas who complains and the woman anoints the *feet* of Jesus.[29] In each of the Gospel chapters narrating the Passover meal, Jesus surprises his disciples by his reversal of their values:

A dispute arose also between them about which should be reckoned the greatest, but he said to them, 'Among pagans it is the kings who lord it over them, and those who have authority over them are given the title Benefactor. This must not happen with you. No; the greatest among you must behave as if he were the youngest, the leader as if he were the one who serves. For who is the greater: the one at table or the one who serves? The one at table, surely? Yet here I am among you as one who serves!['] (Luke 22: 24-27)

Jesus not only reverses the values of his disciples: he changes them for the better – and models this new economy of divine service. This service is significant not only for its action but for its location, the significance of its name and the use of that name in scripture, all of which

---

[28] All scriptural quotation in English from *The Jerusalem Bible* (Jones/1974).
[29] As in Luke 7:36-50 which sets this scene earlier in Christ's ministry.

gives context to Jesus' reply which otherwise sounds unfeeling towards the poor – and to his serving role which so confused his glory-seeking disciples.

> Jesus knew that the Father had put everything into his hands, and that he had come from God and was returning to God, and he got up from table, removed his outer garment and, taking a towel, wrapped it round his waist; he then poured water into a basin and began to wash the disciples' feet and to wipe them with the towel he was wearing. He came to Simon Peter, who said to him, 'Lord, are you going to wash my feet?' Jesus answered, 'At the moment you do not understand what I am doing but later you will understand'. (John 13:3-7)

A possible meaning of the name of this village, Bethany, *beth-ani*, is 'House of the Poor'. *Ani*, or *Ana*, can have many meanings in Hebrew including 'humiliation' or 'oppression' and it is this that Hannah complains of in the 1st Book of Samuel, and both she and Mary (in her song in the Gospel of Luke) rejoice that the Lord has looked on them in their lowliness. The Gospel of Luke also contains the account of the Ascension of Jesus for which the words of Hannah and Mary provide a context and a meaning.

Bethany is outside Jerusalem because that is where the lepers, the poorest of the poor, had to live. That is where Jesus dines, in solidarity, that is where Jesus is anointed and that is where Jesus ascends into heaven.

In the Gospel, which turns the world upside-down, Jesus enters the Kingdom of God from precisely the place of the most dire poverty – because that is the only way in – he ascends into glory from the place of humiliation and oppression. At a time when the world needed to remember Mary's words that *he has pulled down princes from their thrones*, Dietrich Bonheoffer reminded Christians that earthly powers, earthly leaders, princes and parliaments do not command their final allegiance – that duty is primarily to God. And so, states may serve the poor and needy because of their need or in order to control them – but Christians are bound to serve those who are poor and those who are in need because they recognise in them a human dignity that is divinely affirmed.

How might this reversal of values translate in a secular setting? If accounts of metaphysical reality and social situations are so oppressive to women, how might they be changed? The next chapter provides an answer and delves deeper into the trouble with transgender and with incoherent assertions of reality.

8 – The trouble with transgender

Some years ago, in a pub on Great Western Road in Glasgow, I was having a drink with about eight workmates from the multilingual booking line of a famous hotel company. I can't remember why we were in the West End rather than in the city centre where we worked, nor why one of our number (a rather hearty young man, fond of his beer) had absented himself from our table next to the window. I remember clearly the moment when he returned to stand by our table, bringing with him a beautiful and androgynous person whom he introduced in this manner:

> This is Sam, and, guess what? He used to be a woman!

We all sat there with our mouths opening and closing and I can't recall anyone saying anything at all. I know I didn't. It wasn't that the concept was alien to me, one of my boyfriends had been transsexual, but rather that I had no idea how to respond to such an introduction. I can still see Sam's face, clearly disconcerted and surprised that (I imagine) an invitation to 'come and meet my workmates' had terminated in such a crass show and tell.

I have no idea what prompted my workmate to out Sam in this manner, nor what the content of their previous conversation had been. Having lived in various countries where sexuality is variously imagined, I get very annoyed with the macho scenario of some guy chatting me up at a party to the point where I admit that, yes, I have had boyfriends, only to puff out his scrawny chest in triumph, proclaim himself 'straight as a die' and proceed to out me to everyone else present. It's happened many times.

I also recall some years previously meeting a female acquaintance (who had gone out with an ex of mine so may have been harbouring some ambiguous feeling towards me) when, after decades of avoiding football pitches, I had just played a game with an LGBT-friendly team and found the experience both invigorating and healing. Pint glass in hand (she'd clearly had a few) she turned round to her mates, all fellow teachers, and announced:

> This is Alan, and, guess what? He's just played football with a gay team!

So I should have known better. That time it was me who was surprised and disconcerted, and her colleagues who didn't know what to say at such an introduction. I know that, on both occasions, a hearty welcome would have been in order but when one is so conscious of another's vulnerability the last thing one wishes is to subject them to more of the public glare.

I'm ashamed that I made no other response to Sam, whose response to us was to *slip through the crowd and walk away*. I'm proud that I told off my acquaintance, reminding her that it's my choice how to present myself, not hers. I didn't similarly remonstrate with my workmate as I had no wish for him to continue with the subject – and possibly involve Sam in any more upset.

The feelings of cisgender people about transgender people may vary considerably – from identification or solidarity to indifference or repugnance – however they are all around them (if they open their eyes) and demand at least a recognition of our common humanity as well as a manner of approach based on common civility. They would benefit also from greater understanding, not least because of the very real threats they face to their lives and wellbeing:

From verbal harassment to threats of violence, from acts of discrimination to the destruction of property, from assaults to even murder – people who are (or who are perceived as) transgender often face a hostile social climate. Violent behaviour is an estimated four times higher for transgender individuals when compared with the national average (Koken, Bambi, & Parson 2009); NCAVP 2008). Transgender people are more likely to experience hostile or aggressive familial interaction, more likely to be kicked out of their homes by parents, more likely to become homeless or live below the poverty line, and less likely to be employed (Gehi & Arkles 2007); Koken et al. 2009; Xavier 2006). These compounding factors are likely to result in limited health care access, familial aid, and other resources, and to increase the risk of harassment, discrimination, and violence (Stotzer 2009).
(Beemyn & Rankin/2011/90-91)

My first reason to include this long quote by Genny Beemyn and Susan Rankin, from *The Lives of Transgender People*, is that Christians are not known for our embrace of transgender people – disgracefully we are instead infamous for our fear and rejection of them. I am quite aware that many traditional Christians feel that secular forces are silencing their voices, that freedom of conscience is curtailed along with freedom of speech and that religious freedom has barely been attempted, and always and everywhere is subject to the machinations of the State.

I do not dispute any of this, and yet I say that people who are (or who are perceived as) transgender deserve our sympathy – if not as prophets of a new order of justice then at very least as recipients of our compassion, which is mandatory for all those who encounter oppression.

Similarly, radical second wave feminists are also striving to make the world a better, safer, more just place. Like many traditional Christians, some of them now experience the political frustration of no-platforming and silencing (Jeffreys/2014/54-57) and their interventions for women are taken as hatred and fear of trans people:

> Gender, in the form of transgenderism, hurts in many ways that do not just pertain to transgenders themselves. It hurts the wives, partners and family members of men and women who transgender, causing acute distress and loss so severe that some researchers are prepared to call this post-traumatic stress disorder. It hurts, too, the feminist movement, and threatens the gains feminists fought for in the creation of women-only services and spaces. The very few women-only spaces that still exist, such as the Michigan Womyn's Music Festival, are subjected to campaigns of bullying and intimidation. It undermines and causes huge confusion in feminist academia and feminist theory, to the extent that the biological reality of women's lives, on the basis of which, and through which, females are relegated to subordinate status is disappeared, relegated like the dinosaur to history and museums. (Jeffreys/2014/184)

Although Sheila Jeffreys references studies on psychological and physical harm from transgender surgery and hormone treatment (Jeffreys/2014/62-79, chapter written with Lorene Gottschalk) she is not in favour, at all, of traditional binary categories of gender. She has that much in common with Judith Butler. Rather, she expresses concern that the phenomenon of transgender, by policing gender roles and 'normalising'[30] same-sex relationships, directly or indirectly harms lesbians (*op. cit.*/102-109) and gay men (*op. cit.*/32-34) and encourages eugenics (*op. cit.*/123-141).

Pat Califia, who describes herself as a 'genetic female'[31] takes issue with transactivist Kate Bornstein's gender abolitionist agenda: 'Despite its eloquence, Bornstein's view of the power dynamics between men and women is simplistic' (Califia/1997/250). Nevertheless, it is difficult not to feel some sympathy for Bornstein's analysis:

> In the either/or gender class system that we call male and female, the structure of one-up, one-down fulfils the requisite for a power imbalance. It became clear that the reason that the reason that the bipolar gender system continues to exist, and is actively and tenaciously held in place, is that the bi-polar gender system is primarily a venue for the playing out of a power game. It's an arena in which roughly half the people in the world can have power over the other half.

---

[30] Meaning that, after gender transition, same-sex relationships are erased by appearing to conform to socially-imposed normative heterosexuality. Of course it can be argued that the reverse is also true, when other-sex relationships appear to convert to same-sex. Where there is greater acceptance of gender-fluidity, such as is the case in left-wing circles influenced by Queer politics *at the moment*, there is less policing of gender.

[31] Alternative to the prefix 'cis', *i.e.* not 'trans'. The author is now Patrick Califia, the book, *Sex Changes: Transgender Politics* (2003).

Without the structure of the bi-polar gender system, the power dynamic between men and women shatters. People would not have gender to use as a hierarchical framework, and nearly half the members of the bipolar gender system would probably be at a loss. ...I think that male privilege is the glue that holds the system together.[32]

Even as a genetic male, supposedly enjoying a privileged position in this hierarchy, I am sure I am not alone in having experienced the stress of the failed attempt, growing up in a highly gendered community, to be accepted as 'a real boy'. This stress is in no way comparable to the damage and danger experienced by those who are taken as women, genetic females or not. It is more akin to the ongoing gender policing, internal and external, of heterosexual genetic males – which is why so many of them form bonds of friendship (often very affectionate) with homosexual and bisexual genetic males from whom they expect to have their supposedly comparatively stronger masculinity affirmed. Even if that affirmation takes an erotic turn.

Pat Califia, who identifies here as lesbian, is aware of the resistance of gay and bisexual cisgendered men and women to a gender abolitionist agenda when they have dedicated considerable energy into affirming their respective gender status in the face of its widespread, life-long, subtle or brutal rejection by heterosexuals. Both Bornstein and Califia are aware of the consequences for pre-op transsexuals of the dual negation of gender

---

[32] Bornstein/1994/107-108, cited in Califia/1997/250 – with the spellings 'bipolar' and 'bi-polar' reproduced here. Ellipsis Califia.

dysphoria as a mental illness and of the identity of (for example) the post-op gender status of a genetic male with that a cisgender genetic female. If people do not present themselves to a doctor as 'trapped in the wrong gendered body', there is little chance of obtaining hormones or surgery. If, post-op, they do not present themselves to the media as content with their bodily appearance and function, there is less chance of others getting them:

> The demedicalization of transsexualism is a dilemma. There is a demand for genital surgery, largely as a result of the cultural genital imperative. Due to financial requirements, the fulfilment of the surgical dream is subject to cultural and class constraints; cosmetic and genital conversion surgery is available primarily to the middle and upper classes. Transsexuals, especially middle-class pre-operative transsexuals, are heavily invested in maintaining their status as "diseased people". The demedicalization of transsexuality would further limit surgery in this culture, as it would remove the label of "illness" and so prohibit insurance companies from footing the bill. [33]

Califia's response to this is one of ideological anxiety:

> [Bornstein's] genderless and anti-gender stance is not a strong platform from which to argue with transphobes who'd like to keep gender dysphoric people firmly in the bodies and

---

[33] Bornstein/1994/120-122, cited in Califia/1997/260-261. The social class system referred to is that pertaining in the USA.

identities   they   were   born   with.
(Califia/1997/261)

Yet not all resistance to a diagnosis of gender dysphoria is transphobic. Lisa Selin Davis writes in the *New York Times* of the constant questioning of her daughter's gender by well-meaning teachers and other authority figures who assume she has gender dysphoria:

> She is not gender nonconforming. She is gender role nonconforming. She does not fit into the mold that we adults – who have increasingly eschewed millennium-old gender roles ourselves, as women work outside the home and men participate in the domestic sphere – still impose on our children. [...] Somehow, as we have broadened our awareness of and support for gender nonconformity, we've narrowed what we think a boy or girls can look like and do. (Davis/2017)

This situation reminds me of the dynamics of a family known to me whose son's perceived effeminacy prompted his very self-consciously liberal parents to prepare (rather impatiently) for his 'coming out' as gay. When instead he announced that he had 'got his girlfriend pregnant', and that they were going to stay together and raise the baby jointly, they were rather disconcerted!

My concerns in regard to people who are (or who are perceived as) transgender are: their fragility in the face of prejudice; the scarring and sterility which attend physical gender transition, often chosen (or chosen by parents) at an inappropriately young age for a life-changing and irreversible decision; their relationships with feminists, with lesbians, gay men and bisexual people; the loss of at least some sexual function and capacity for pleasure, and their safety in society and the courage and loneliness which, in the present climate, seem to be a usual part of their lives.

In the face of all this, a coherent theory of the human person which manages to articulate the experience currently referred to as sex and gender may make some contribution to the possibility of a common language for people who sincerely uphold the values of equality and diversity.

Thus far we have seen that there are many competing philosophical and theoretical discourses which aim to describe the human person – and some which go further and attempt to describe existence. As a philosopher and theologian, one of my concerns regards the inadequacy of the language currently used by transgender people (and their supporters) to describe their experience of reality.

This inadequacy largely stems from the lack of realisation that the attempt to describe reality, and one's experience of it, is in a venerable metaphysical tradition and that in order to be successful it must satisfy more criteria than those of popularity, sympathy or ideological convenience.

So for me to make the statement that, 'I *identify* as a woman', that 'I am *really* a woman', or that 'I am a *real* woman', and to mean more in terms of reality than a statement regarding a role in a play, such as 'I'm Julius Caesar', requires considerable theoretical support – especially if I refuse to provide any medical evidence (or that which is available is contradictory to my statement) and also refuse to accept that the reality I refer to in these statements is purely psychological or imaginary.

I know this may sound incredibly harsh and judgemental. But this is what introducing the words 'real' or 'really' into such discourse does – they become claims about reality, not just about performance of roles. One way out of this is to assert that the reality of gender is no more than a role-play; Judith Butler says it is just that:

> The performance of drag plays upon the distinction of the anatomy of the performer and the gender that is being performed. But we are actually in the presence of three contingent dimensions of significant corporeality: anatomical sex, gender identity and gender performance. If the anatomy of the performer is already distinct from the gender of the performer, and both of those are distinct from the gender of the performance, then the performance suggests a dissonance not only between sex and performance, but sex and gender, and gender and performance. As much as drag creates a unified picture of a "woman" (what its critics often oppose), it also reveals the distinctness of those aspects of gendered experience which are falsely naturalized as a unity (Butler/1999/175)

In other words there's no such thing as 'a natural woman' (or a natural man).[34] Butler sees even the claim to identify anatomical sex as political. She goes further and

_____

[34] Butler (1999/ note 34 to p.28) takes issue with Aretha Franklin for singing that she feels like one (Butler therefore seemingly claiming to understand Franklin's lived experience better that she herself) and with Carly Simon for writing the song *A Natural Woman*.

asserts that there is no possibility of theory on the nature of nature – as all views on reality are politicised.

> There is no ontology of gender on which we might construct a politics, for gender ontologies always operate within established political contexts as normative injunctions, determining what qualifies as intelligible sex, invoking and consolidating the reproductive constraints on sexuality, setting the prescriptive requirements whereby sexed or gendered bodies come into intelligibility. Ontology is, thus, not a foundation, but [...] operates insidiously by installing itself into political discourse as its necessary ground. (Butler/1999/189)

It is important to realise what this shift from rejection of ontology of gender to rejection of ontology in general implies. Butler is not only saying that gender is socially constructed, and that so is sex, but that everything is. If gender theorists repudiate the possibility of any meaningful objective discourse to describe reality, then what meaning can be given to the assertion (of anyone at all) 'I am *really* a woman'? As gender theorists also repudiate the assertion 'I feel like a natural woman', then the short answer is 'none'. The statement, in these theoretical circumstances, is meaningless.

So we are left with several scenarios, with the possibility of various admixtures, as well as local and temporal coincidence, in regard to assertions of gender and transgender:

> 1 globalised traditional gender roles based on globalised traditional sex categories based on a globalised ontology

2 culture-specific traditional gender roles based on culture-specific traditional sex categories based on a culture-specific ontology

3 globalised traditional gender roles based on globalised opposite sex categories based on a strategic repudiation of globalised patriarchy

4 culture-specific nontraditional gender roles based on culture-specific nontraditional sex categories based on a strategic repudiation of culture-specific patriarchy

5 people, wherever and whenever, making up their identity as they go along

This is not an exhaustive list (there is also the possibility of tinkering with roles and categories without repudiating them) but it may bring some clarity to list and compare at least some possibilities. Scenario 1 is the view of traditional Christians, with Scenario 2 the view of the more enlightened missionaries and others who have spent time abroad or in communities of other ethnicity.

Scenario 3 is the context for the assertion made by a person with male anatomy who claims to really be a woman, *or vice-versa*. It is also the location of drag queens, drag kings, screaming queens and stone butch dykes – many of whom make no connections between their performance of stereotypical crossgender attributes and that of the phenomenon of transgender which they see as distinct from these cultural lesbian and gay phenomena.[35]

---

[35] See Jeffreys/2014/14-20 for the appropriation of historic and contemporary lesbian and gay experience by transactivists which she names 'transnapping'. In contrast, is the view of Kate Bornstein (playwright of *The Opposite Sex ...Is Neither!*): 'sex is fucking,

Feminism is currently between this scenario and the next – while scenario 5 is only currently imaginable in science fiction. Note that scenario 3 has no mention of ontology. In this face of this situation, we have two options:

A – to accept that all performance of identity is performative and that therefore there is no underlying reality to assertions about one's sex, gender, race, age, nationality, experience, profession, qualifications or anything else supposedly objective in the universe.

B – to utilise an inter-subjective ontology that is flexible enough to adapt to specific situations and coherent enough to provide for the possibility of reference to a reality existing outside of the mind of an individual.

The next chapter explores what option B might look like.

---

everything else is gender' cited by Shannon Bell (1993/104). Bell elucidates: 'Every lesbian and gay man is transgressing gender roles and gender rules. Whereas not all transgendered people are lesbian and gay, all lesbians and gays are transgendered.' (*op. cit.*/116)

9 – Patterns of value

As Christians turned to the metaphysics of substance of a Classical 'pagan philosopher' they may find a solution to their controversy in the metaphysics of Quality of another: the American philosopher Robert M. Pirsig. Pirsig's first book, *Zen and the Art of Motorcycle Maintenance*, presents his thesis in the form of a novel, 'for rhetorical reasons' (Pirsig/1999/Author's Note) which describes a long motorcycle trip – based on one Pirsig took from Minnesota west with the characters in the book, his friends and his son, Chris. In this book, Pirsig (having rebuilt his life after a nervous breakdown) is not only a keen observer of detail but has turned his inquiring mind away from the obsession with metaphysical problems which nearly destroyed him. He has a belts-and-braces attitude to this pleasure trip, and to technology in general.

Pirsig's friends John and Sylvia are affectionately portrayed as hippies and if he seems to envy their *joie-de-vivre*, he cannot comprehend their hatred of technology. In one incident John floods his engine (by using unnecessary choke) and cannot comprehend why, nor cope with any mechanical explanation by Pirsig. Another time he has loose handlebars but rejects Pirsig's offer of a shim ('a thin, flat strip of metal'[36] – which would help to tighten them) because Pirsig:

> had the *nerve* to propose repair of his new eighteen-hundred dollar BMW, the pride of half a century of German mechanical finesse, with a piece of old *beer* can!

---

[36] Pirsig/1999/57-8. The flooded engine incident is *op. cit.*/20.

[...] beer-can aluminum is soft and sticky, as metals go. Perfect for the application. Aluminum doesn't oxidise in wet weather – or, more precisely, it always has a thin layer of oxide that prevents any further oxidation. Also perfect. (Pirsig/1999/58)

So, as the shim was perfect and would not even be seen, why was John so angry? Pirsig provides an answer to both incidents by commenting on:

why he got upset that day he couldn't get his engine started. It was an *intrusion on his reality*. It just blew a hole through his whole groovy way of looking at things and he would not face up to it because it seemed to threaten his whole life style [...] What you've got here, really, are *two* realities, one of immediate artistic appearance and one of underlying scientific explanation, and they don't match (Pirsig/1999/61, emphasis original)

The last sentence neatly summarises the history of (the components of) reality in Western metaphysics: the empirical or experiential former – Plato and Aristotle's φαινομενα, the scholastic *accidenta*, the dualist *res extensae*, Immanuel Kant's *a posteriori*, F.S.C. Northrop's 'aesthetic continuum' and Pirsig's 'romantic quality'; and the hypothetical or theoretical latter – Ιδεα,[37] *forma*, *res cogitans*, *a priori*, 'theoretic component', 'classical quality', respectively (with much borrowing and confusion).

---

[37] See discussion on Socrates/ Plato/ Aristotle and Ideal lexis in Ross/1924/160-1.

Aristotle developed Plato's thought (as Plato did Socrates') which eventually led to their quite fundamental disagreement. His marriage of the Platonic Ideal and the mundane material was by use of the traditionally-named 'Four Causes'.

To return to the motorcycle for illustration: its End is its destination/ purpose in the plan of the Prime Mover, God. Its Efficient Cause is. petrol, which supplies the motive force. Its Material Cause is metal and its Formal Cause the Idea MOTORCYCLE. I simplify the Causes greatly and they could also be illustrated (rather facetiously) as: it's meant; it goes; it's tangible; and it's real!

The combination of the last two mark the difference with Plato: this motorcycle is no mere shadow of a truly existent Idea. It is formed by this Idea but it is real. The 'substance' of this motorcycle is, apart from the sensory 'accidents' of colour, smell, texture, sounds (and taste), an amorphous piece of the omnipresent *'prima materia'* prime matter which Pirsig dismisses as having none of the proofs of existence.[38]

Zen and the Art of Motorcycle Maintenance develops Pirsig's first philosophical move: 'at the moment of pure Quality, there is no subject and there is no object.' (Pirsig/1999/290) This synthesis of Quality he equates with the famous Sanskrit maxim *'tat tvam asi'*, this is that (*ibid*). Much of this book concerns relationships: with technology and between people. Developing Pirsig's thought, I describe Quality as 'harmonious relationship' and state that we are constituted by our relationships.

This metaphysics accords with the theories of the New Physics, explained by Murray Gell-Mann, the Nobel

---

[38] See discussion on Hume and Kant, Pirsig/1999/130-137.

laureate physicist who named the quark, who sees relationships as the fundamental components of reality:

> Superstring theory grew out of an idea called the bootstrap principle [...] the particles, if assumed to exist, produce forces binding them to one another, the resulting bound states are the same particles, and they are the same as the ones carrying the forces. (Gell-Mann/1994/128)

He explains superstring theory in musical terms:

> A good analogy is with a violin string, which has a lowest mode of vibration and an infinite number of other modes (harmonics) of higher and higher musical frequency. But in quantum mechanics energy is like frequency multiplied by Planck's constant h. The particles of the low-mass sector can be visualised as the lowest modes of the various sorts of loops of string occurring in superstring theory, while particles with masses comparable to the fundamental unit of mass represent the next-lowest modes, and still heavier particles represent higher modes, and so on forever. (Gell-Mann/1994/203,204)

Although the propositions of physics and metaphysics are not identical, they should be at least compatible. Not compatible with Newton, Pirsig's metaphysics does seem to be compatible with quantum mechanics. Pirsig asserts: 'Substance is a subspecies of value' (Pirsig/1992/124). However:

> as John Locke pointed out in the seventeenth century, if we ask what this substance is, devoid of any properties, we find ourselves thinking of

nothing whatsoever. The data of quantum physics indicate that what are called 'subatomic particles' cannot possibly fill the definition of a substance. The properties exist, then disappear, then exist, and then disappear again in little bundles called 'quanta'. These bundles are not continuous in time, yet an essential, defined characteristic of 'substance' is that it *is* continuous in time […] it follows that there is no substance anywhere in the world nor has there ever been.[39]

He concludes: 'Strike out the word 'substance' wherever it appears and substitute the expression 'stable inorganic pattern of value.'' (Pirsig/1992/128) Which is a similar answer to the problem of causation:

To say that 'A *causes* B' or to say that 'B *values* precondition A' is to say the same thing […] Instead of saying 'A magnet *causes* iron filings to move towards it,' you can say 'Iron filings *value* movement toward a magnet.' […] The only difference between causation and value is that the word 'cause' implies absolute certainty whereas the implied meaning of 'value' is one of preference […] An individual particle is not absolutely committed to one predictable behaviour. What appears to be an absolute cause is just a very consistent pattern of preferences.[40]

Pirsig substitutes 'stable patterns of value' for 'substance' and 'values' for 'causes' (both as verbs). We

---

[39] Pirsig/1992/127-128, emphasis original.
[40] Pirsig/1992/126-127, emphasis original.

can conclude that, as beings, we co-create the cosmos – by what we value. The relationships which constitute us, constitute the universe; as beings value other beings. The values of individual relationships accord with some other relationships but are discordant with yet others.

String theory harmonises with much of the spiritual ontology that has been thrown out from the Enlightenment on. And it must be said that neither Plato nor Pythagoras would admit Music to be less of a fundamental science than Physics. Μουσική (*musiké*) comprised both – and also Philosophy.

I agree with Pirsig that Quality neither inheres solely in the subject nor in the object, but rather than 'event' (Pirsig/1999/239), I believe Quality to be harmony. Pirsig, in fact, mentions harmony and uses it to describe 'classic beauty', basing this on the observations of an 'astronomer, a physicist, a mathematician and philosopher' (Pirsig/1999/259) Henri Jules Poincaré.

Pirsig (*op.cit.*/268) restricts his use of the word 'harmony' to describe Classical aesthetics – the proportions of a statute or the elegance of a mathematical formula. I would venture to say that the terms 'proportion' or 'symmetry' would be more apt here – if there is the need to make this restriction – but I feel this is unnecessary. Pirsig speaks of 'classic beauty, which comes from the harmonious ordering of the parts, and which a pure intelligence can grasp, which gives structure to romantic beauty' (*ibid*).

I agree. Although I have no idea what a 'pure intelligence' is and I doubt Pirsig meant an angel. Yet, when musicians can cause an audience to clap, to weep and to stand up and dance; what moves us is not simply the nice maths of the chords – but it is certainly harmony.

The harmony between our experience of the music and our past, between us and the musicians, between their performance and their emotions and between themselves and between each of us and each other. The Classical Greek understanding of this all-embracing harmony still echoes in the word 'arithmetic': 'number' in Greek is αριθμός (*arithmos*) – from the same root as 'rhythm'.

I have followed Pirsig as my guide thus far and I mean to continue. However I feel his metaphysical synthesis of the 'Classic'/'Romantic' dualism which he observed in his first work, is even more elegant if 'harmony' is not only Classical but also Romantic. Idea and experience, form and content, subject and object, order and symmetry and aesthetics and emotion: harmony is all and between all.

So fundamental reality is composed of music: of harmonies of superstrings reverberating, sustaining and resolving – the whole cosmos a resounding network of relationships from supercluster to organism to sub-atomic wave-particle. In this paradigm, God could not be more involved with us – and yet is still transcendent.

If God is 'nearer to us than our jugular vein' (as *Surah* 50:16 of the *Qur'an* states) if 'in Him we live and move and have our being' (Acts 17:22-28) then even the most transcendent concept of the divine, in religions based on monotheism and revelation, admits communication and perhaps communion but certainly relationship.

However this does not imply pantheism. God in this paradigm is the quality of Goodness in all relationships and this existence is real. The Holy Trinity may therefore be described as the paradigm of all inter-subjective reality: Love loving Love. All other beings are the confluence of their relationships but God is not this: God is the greater harmony into which all consonance and dissonance resolve. This implies that the concepts of 'before' and 'outside' in relation to God and the space-time continuum have no meaning.[41] It is not that the creation contains the Creator but rather, conversely, that the spheres – from atom to star – have always been in harmony. The metaphysics is Pirsig's and the theology mine, although it is not original.

Clement of Alexandria, in his 'Exhortation to the Greeks'[42] (Butterworth/1919) calls Christ 'minstrel' (*op.cit.*/9), 'new music' (*op.cit.*/7), 'new song' (*ibid*) and uses the word αρμονίας (harmony) for 'music'.

Despite Richard Dawkins' misquote of Pirsig in *The God Delusion*;[43] rather than anti-religious, Pirsig is concerned by the tendency for social values to attempt to appropriate intellectual values. An ascending scale of values is not a new thought, as Pirsig admits in his second book, *Lila*, a meditation not this time by road but by river, where he develops a hierarchy of moral value from the inanimate to the biological, social and intellectual.

A similar classification to Pirsig's: 'the vegetative, the sensitive and the rational' (Boehner & Laughlin/1955/61) is taken for granted by St. Bonaventure, in the 13th Century, whose thought Boehner and Laughlan (1955/61) explain, in what could almost be a quote from Pirsig:

> The rational powers are higher than the sensitive
> powers and exercise sway over them; the latter,
> in turn, are higher than the vegetative powers.

[41] Yet the Creator is not dependent upon the creation. See Sokolowski/2006/61.

[42] Butterworth (1919/2-263) The odd pages are Clement's Greek, with Butterworth's English facing on the even pages.

[43] Dawkins/2007/28, (Pirsig quote unreferenced). *Cf.* Pirsig/1992/383-384.

The order of their generation, however, is the reverse. The vegetative powers build and sustain the sentient organisms by which the activities of sensitive life are exercised.

'Almost' because, as well as the change from 'sensitive' to 'social', Pirsig does not hold with the statement directly preceding the above quote: 'These grades of life function in perfect harmony' (Boehner & Laughlin/1955/61) but rather states that:

> This classification of patterns is not very original, but the Metaphysics of Quality allows an assertion about them that is unusual: it says they are not continuous. They are discreet [...] Although each higher level is built on a lower level it is not an extension of that lower level. Quite the contrary. The higher level can often be seen to be in opposition to the lower level, dominating it, controlling it where possible for its own purposes. (Pirsig/1992/179)

As Pirsig alters previous hierarchies, so I alter his. Pirsig (1992/350) sees intelligence (in terms of discernment of high and low quality) operating at all levels therefore I feel a more exact designation of the level of static patterns of value which immediately transcends the socio-personal is 'imaginary'. I mean that here intelligence is abstract.

I use the term socio-personal as I consider the personal and the social to be two different but overlapping configurations of our identity. I feel that my school social role as the academic educator called Dr. McManus; and my personal identity as Alan, are not as qualitatively different as are my molecules, my cells and my thoughts. Our social and personal patterns of value are differing configurations of the same level of reality. So I expand Pirsig's scheme:

Starting with the LUDIC, where the play of patterns and values is unstable or unmanifest, I follow Pirsig's logic of Dynamic Quality transcending this level of reality and forming a better one: *atomic & molecular bonding* lead to the INORGANIC (which I prefer to 'inanimate') *carbon bonding* results in the BIOLOGICAL, *sex & kinship* in the SOCIO-PERSONAL, *strategy & semiotics* in the IMAGINARY, a *leap of faith* in the SPIRITUAL and finally *mysticism* leading to some reality where all things, all patterns are valued...and therefore none are and we are back at the luminous potential of the LUDIC level.

I congratulate you for your stamina in having read so far. I realise that reading a book that promises a theoretical solution to two sometimes very antagonistic debates, and keeps delaying delivery, must require considerable patience. Which is a virtue. And, in the charming words of the bookmark of St Teresa, obtains all that it strives for. May it be so!

The next chapter expounds a possibility for conceptualising the Eucharist which may be acceptable to both Catholic and Reformed Christians alike.

61

10 – A new song

Thomas Aquinas, at first controversially, rather than the ideas of 'the Divine Plato' turned to 'the pagan philosopher' Aristotle, in whose understanding of ουσία (essence or substance) and φαινομενα (phenomena) he found an elegant explanation of the Eucharist: the substance of Christ and the appearance of bread. To scholastics such as Aquinas this division between *essentia* and *accidenta* was not counter-intuitive. However it *was* complex. Moloney details 'the classic account of transubstantiation':

> What then happens to the accidents of the bread and wine once their entire substantial reality has been changed? Clearly the accidents remain unchanged, as our senses make abundantly manifest, but in a unique situation. Ordinarily accidents inhere in a subject. In this case the previous subject exists no more. Does this mean that the accidents inhere in the substance of Christ? The answer must be negative, since that would expose Christ's body to material change in a way that would contradict his glorified state. Thomas's account of this obscure point maintains that the accidents exist without a subject, but that the accident of quantity acts as a 'quasi-subject' for the rest. Consequently, when I bite the host, it is this 'quasi-subject' which is being bitten, not, strictly speaking, the body of Christ. [...] For Thomas the role previously exercised by the respective substances is now taken over by the power of God working through the original miracle of transubstantiation. The

accidents are maintained in being and activity through the divine action itself.[44] The principal cause is God, but this action is mediated through the substance of Christ into which the previous substances have been changed by the original miracle. (Moloney/1995/144-145, paraphrasing 'Aquinas, ST III, q.79, aa.3-6')

Butler is also interested in the absence of substance but explicitly rejects the notion of accidents (in her language, 'dissonant adjectives') acting as a quasi-substance:

> It is of course always possible to argue that dissonant adjectives work retroactively to redefine the substantive identities they are said to modify and, hence, to expand the substantive categories of gender to include possibilities that they previously excluded. But if these substances are nothing other than the coherences contingently created through the regulation of attributes, it would seem that the ontology of substances itself is not only an artificial effect, but essentially superfluous. (Butler/1999/33)

---

[44] The accident of quantity is unique, according to Aristotle, as it is the only one possessed by matter in general rather than by a particular substance: "essence depends upon quality, and this is of a determinate, whereas quantity is of an indeterminate nature" (Ross/1924/80-81). The Greek word here translated as 'quality' is ποιόν (*poión*) which may also be rendered as 'attribute'; 'essence' translates οὐσία (*oúsía*) which is often translated as 'substance'. The term 'essence' is sometimes invoked in support of gender identity – see Jeffreys (2014/30-32) on feminine essence theory and Gatens (1991/48-59) of the rejection of the related concept, the 'eternal feminine', by Simone de Beauvoir in her famous feminist existential analysis of gender relations, *The Second Sex*.

My critique of the social construction of reality is firstly that it is speciesist – meaning that the only society which is taken as meaningful is the human (generally White, middle-class and academic). In my first book on 'the nature of nature', I took issue with the famous question of undergraduate lecture halls:

> If a tree falls in the forest, and there's nobody there to see it, does it *really* fall? [...] The question annoys me because it assumes that all this activity and upheaval depends entirely on the possibility of it being perceived by whatever member of the human species is anti-social enough to be wandering about forests in the hope of seeing trees fall! [...] But what's unhealthy about this question, in terms of intellectual health, is that sneaky little word '*really*'.
>
> Because it does two things – the first so sneakily that we hardly notice: it totally ignores the perception of the squirrel who was just about to jump from the neighbouring tree, the perception of the fledglings falling out of their nest who are having their first experience of flight, the perception of all the ants who were marching up the trunk and suddenly find themselves marching sideways, the perception of the chlorophyll sensors on the blades of grass which moments ago were in sunlight.
>
> In ignoring the existence and the perception of all these creatures, this immoral philosophy question does a great disservice not only to them but also to their creator.
>
> But that's not the only sneaky thing about this word that sneaked into the sentence like I

sneaked into the lecture. The word *'really'* implies that what you see might be what you get – but it ain't what's there. Not *really*. So then, it implies that there's a whole other dimension of reality behind all the bangs and crashes and fright. (McManus/2013/73-75)

Although the spiritual dimension may be optional for many of the Butler's readers, it is not for those attempting to work out an ecumenical understanding of the Eucharist. My metaphysical addition of the Spiritual level (transcending the intellectual or Imaginary) is because I consider the attempted classification of all religious reality as either social, intellectual or mystical to be inadequate. There exists a huge literature and rich lived experience of a stable state of being which is not totally comprised of good deeds, contemplation of intellectual verities, or rapture. Pirsig is aware of this when commenting on Zen ritual:

You would guess from the literature on Zen and its insistence on discovering the 'unwritten *dharma*' that it would be intensely anti-ritualistic, since ritual is the 'written *dharma*'. But that isn't the case. The Zen monk's daily life is nothing but one ritual after another, hour after hour, day after day, all his life. They don't tell him to shatter those static patterns to discover the unwritten *dharma*. They want him to get those patterns perfect! [...] You free yourself from static patterns by putting them to sleep. [...] Phædrus saw nothing wrong with this ritualistic religion as long as the rituals are seen as merely a static portrayal of Dynamic Quality, a sign-post which allows socially pattern-

dominated people to see Dynamic Quality. The danger has always been that the rituals, the static patterns, are mistaken for what they represent and are allowed to destroy the Dynamic Quality they were originally intended to preserve.
(Pirsig 1992/447-448, emphasis original)

Bread, wine, Passover, paschal lamb, papal pronouncements, religious reforms and metaphysical schemes; all are static patterns of value. The Spirit of God, as Dynamic Quality, has pulsated within all patterns since the beginning: creating, destroying, inspiring and transcending them. The whole and entire self of Christ and the substance of the bread and wine are not equivalent. They cannot be considered in the same class, like two tenants in a house or two ghosts in a machine.

In his small, carefully-worded and rather convoluted work on the subject, the solution of the RC Dutch Dominican theologian Edward Schillebeeckx is mostly named 'transignification' – but on careful reading appears in broad terms to be a return to Platonic realism (*i.e.* idealism). This otherworldy creed has poisoned Christianity since the conversion of St Augustine of Hippo as it is a denial of the full reality of God's creation as stated boldly from the beginning sentence of the Book of Genesis through every ecumenical creed until the present day. Added to the pernicious influence of Manichaeanism, also the gift of Augustine, the adoption of this world-denying heresy has led Christians to the denigration of nature, the body, material goods, sex and sexuality and of all their embodiments (all women, queer and transgender people chief among them) – clearing the way for the colonial demonizing of animism and for the destruction of the intricate ecological relationships which it revered.

So I don't really feel that it helps! I know I am far too harsh on *The Eucharist*, which provides a very helpful account of the dogmatic deliberations before, during and after the bulwark of Counter-Reformation that was the Council of Trent, so to balance my judgement I will say that Schillebeeckx's inclusion of another term for Eucharistic change, from 'the ancient Eastern [Greek] liturgies [:] *metarrythmizesthai*' (Schillebeeckx/1968/66) is metaphysically very interesting.

The Pythagorean concept of *arithmos* – as mystical, musical and mathematical value – encapsulates the all-inclusive harmony which composes creation. So rather than vainly attempting to imagine some finite yet indeterminate solid substance (*prima materia* spread out will-nilly with *secunda materia* dolloped in specific species – with nary a quality among them) we may understand my Pirsigian paradigm of patterns of value by means of a Pythagorean metaphor of music.

John Powell, in *How Music Works*, explains that a musical note differs from 'non-musical noises' in that it 'is made up of a ripple pattern which repeats itself over and over again' (Powell/2010/22) and that it 'consists of four things: a loudness, a duration, a timbre and a pitch' (*op. cit.*/6). His (hilarious) account of 'perfect pitch' makes clear that this aspect of music, like the others, is an inter-subjective experience of patterns of value.[45] Those are *my* words. *His* are that the notes used to construct this concept 'are only correct because someone had to decide how long flutes and other wind instruments should be' (*op. cit.*/10) and that these notes were 'chosen by a committee in 1939' (*op. cit.*/16).

---

[45] See Sokolowski/2006/205.

Theologians with more musical knowledge that I may play with this metaphor of the quaternity of values composing patterns of harmony and dissonance. This may become especially relevant when we consider Eucharistic change and presence as transposition.

Christ appropriates the patterned values of bread and wine, as a musician takes up a tune and makes it into a symphony; by re-valuing the elements, bringing them into harmony, into the New Song which is his whole and entire self. A song which is perceived by faith.

Scripture itself answers concerns about priestly magic or Christ's presence being dependent upon the faith of the believer: 'faith is the substance of things hoped for; the evidence of things unseen.' (Heb 11:1). God is both the fount from which faith springs and the sea into which it returns. Inasmuch as Christians have faith, they may encounter Christ in the Eucharist. Christians have faith, inasmuch as God wills it.

Inter-subjectively, believers encounter Christ really present, as their faith and hope accord with his love. The elements of bread and wine change as they are revalued by the believing community as a whole, transposed and taken up into the Eucharistic mystery of the mystical body of Christ.

This metaphor of transposition, with resultant new harmonies and dissonance, is further explored in the following chapter which presents a theory of the human person that may be useful for radical second wave feminists and transactivists in their search for a common language – and may, incidentally, be intelligible to Christians who feel threatened (or outraged) by increasing calls for inclusive education comprising ever-wider topics of gender and sexuality.

11 – Being and becoming

On being [46]

In the venerable discipline of Zen Buddhism, patterns of value (though not named as such) are only to be taken seriously in order to enable sufferers of *karma* to escape their apparent reality. The luminous emptiness which is the Void, is the only 'real' reality.

In the metaphysics I propose, based on my reading of Pirsig, the ludic level is certainly real and fundamental, and 'luminous emptiness' is perhaps a good way to describe it. However the patterns of value which make up the other levels are also real, and not less so. This can be seen from a foundational text of Western culture, the Book of Genesis, when reviewing the creation of each day: 'and God saw that it was good' (וירא אלהים כי־טוב).[47] Even the most Zen-like religious concepts – the *Ein Soph*, the Cloud of Unknowing, the *Nada, Nada, Nada* of St. John of the Cross – even these pinnacles of iconoclasm do not deny creation, based as it is upon value: not illusory, not neutral, but good.

Value is also the basis of the procession of static quality (inorganic – biological – social – intellectual – spiritual) a scale upon which to weigh our actions. This deliberation is necessary – as the 'ends' of the transformation of patterns of values are as controversial as the explanation of the means. Value is the union of the Good and the True, therefore this procession is at the same time a moral hierarchy and a system of epistemological categories.

---

[46] Some material for this section is taken from my doctoral thesis: McManus/2011/239-244.

[47] Genesis 1:12, with variations for each Day.

This scheme clarifies the confusing creed (*de rigueur* among faithful followers of Foucault and Butler) that sexuality is socially constructed and ideas are in some way 'inscribed upon the body' (Foucault/1990/106) and also explains why the terms 'mind' and especially 'soul' are, in academia, generally *anathema*. It qualifies the silly educational slogan: 'all learning is social'. Learning occurs on all levels of reality and so, strangely enough, some learning is intellectual! It also clarifies the 'common sense' assumption of the beneficial effect, on one's mood, of the satisfaction of biological urges.

One recently bereaved is usually encouraged by family and friends to take adequate rest, eat heartily and to exercise. The bereaved person (I speak from personal experience) may doubt the need to attend to any of these urges and yet, after being gently but firmly coerced, may say: 'I needed that'. This common phrase is the mental recognition of these necessities, now satisfied, which the distressed mind has previously ignored. This biological satisfaction may not appear to comfort that mind but at least it removes another strong source of stress and therefore affords some relief – the beneficial effect derives from the analogous relationship of biological and emotional lack and provision.

Thus it would seem that the common sense assumption (that a lower level of quality can influence a higher) is vindicated and that the automatic transmission of value from any level of quality, upward, is obvious. However there is a contrary case. Victims of sexual abuse report that one of the most painful processes of their recovery is letting go of the guilt and shame they feel when their body has reacted sexually to the assault.[48]

From a Pirsigian perspective, the disjuncture of each level of quality with each other is not unexpected – he describes them as 'discreet' (Pirsig/1992/179). In the case of sexual abuse the biological value of the act of penetration is not in harmony with socio-personal values.

The act of physically comforting the bereaved person is also valued differently on the biological and socio-personal levels, however, in this case, these values are in harmony. What the attentive family and friends are attempting is the conscious transformation of a pattern of value from a state of lesser to greater well-being. I do not say 'level' but state. I am not suggesting we convert biological beings into pure intelligences or attempt to quicken the dead. I am however suggesting that operations carried out on one level will affect another. Common sense accepts that such a transformation is possible when a superior pattern of value (e.g. a mood) is affected by an inferior (e.g. a meal).

However – contrary to 'common sense' – the reverse is also true: the intellectual level can, in some circumstances, affect the biological. If I announced to a class of teenagers in a large multicultural comprehensive that science had proven empirically that there is no intrinsic difference in IQ, morality and health between Black people and White, I doubt my announcement would cause much of a stir.

In 1963, when the audience at the steps of the Lincoln Memorial heard this same idea, phrased in the powerful rhetoric of Rev. Martin Luther King, mouths gasped, hearts beat faster and eyes overflowed with tears. I could read his speech out word-for-word and not get that effect

---

[48] See Bass & Davis/1997.

now. His dream, his idea, transformed the socio-personal level, liberating relationships from the constraints of apartheid; and this new reality, dynamic and explosive, liberated too heavy hearts, bated breath and repressed tears.[49]

Critical theorists are not all wrong. Although not identical, the biological is closely connected to the socio-personal level: the humble, eyes-averted slouch (accompanied by avoidance of blame by the appearance of stupidity) which racist Whites expected of oppressed Blacks, is a product of both levels. The following quoted expression, from a 19th century 'Negro Nationalist', in the language of the time, makes this clear:

> Never lacking in compassion for the plight of the slaves, Nationalistic leaders yet remained committed to the belief that the race would not rise to equality in America or, as one man expressed it, that the colored [*sic*] child, "cannot be raised in America without being stoop shouldered".[50]

The social relationships which constitute racism are influenced by (and influence) ideas; but we fail to distinguish between one reality and another if we fail to see that between the racist idea and the oppressed physical

---

[49] See www.etribes.com/bfparker (accessed 05/09/07) for a blow-by-blow account of audience vocal and physical reaction to King's speech of Tuesday 6th December 1955 in Dexter Avenue Baptist Church, Montgomery, Alabama, following the arrest of Rosa Parks.
[50] Bell/1996/103 quotes p.208 of Martin R. Delaney (1852) *The Condition, Elevation, Emigration, and Destiny of the Colored People of the United States. Politically Considered*, King and Baird, Philadelphia, adding 'Delaney is here quoting William Whipper' in the footnote. Gloss is mine.

posture there lies a reality which links philosophy with physiology: if it is helpful to describe the body as being 'inscribed', then the semiotics of that inscription is both social and personal.

Semiotics is precisely the Dynamic Quality which broke out of the socio-personal and formed the basis of the intellectual. However, like changing gears in a car, if relationships of value form patterns from a ludic background then there is no need for any configuration to precede any other. All that *is* necessary is that the values are right.

There is much in common between my personality and my social role but I and others value this commonality differently. To believe otherwise puts me in danger of Orwellian delusions of the total appropriation of the person by the public. Therefore I could re-draw my cyclical procession as a psychedelic palimpsest, each level of a different hue and each superimposed on the others. These levels are all potentially present all the time but some levels may not be constantly manifest – as in the case of a non-dreaming sleeper whose biological level of quality is predominant and whose intellectual level is 'switched off'.

The level which is predominant is that which is valued. The predominance changes as the values change. The reason why I can simultaneously state that the intermediate level between the biological and the intellectual is the socio-personal and that no level necessarily proceeds from another is that personal changes of values tend to manifest socially. There is nothing whatsoever to stop them manifesting intellectually or spiritually – or physically (on the inorganic level) for that matter.

On becoming [51]

This chapter, so far, has largely described being. From this point on it deals with becoming – a key concept in both transubstantiation and transgender. Patterns are precious, they constitute our very reality and we risk chaos when we break out of them, to pursue a 'higher' order. So, why do some beings take this risk? Perhaps it is in our nature as human beings to use our evolutionary impetus to hurl ourselves into an unknown future. Indeed each level of reality may be viewed as an emergent quality made manifest by a particular configuration of the level that it is based on.

It is this emergent relationship which *tends* to influence an adjacent superior level. An example is the socio-personal change that occurred to me after a biological transformation: I'd practiced the balletic Brazilian martial art of *capoeira* for years in Brazil and Spain but, on return to Scotland to study, the Sports Union President dismissed my application to found a university *capoeira* club on the grounds that it was a 'Mickey Mouse sport's club' (*i.e.* of low social and biological value). I persisted, attracted members, practiced regularly and became lithe and athletic. At the end of the year I was seen on campus – for the first time in my life – as a 'sporty' person and he recommended that I ask my club members to nominate me for a sporting 'Blue' award.

The pursuit of health, holiness, happiness or Quality is both valuable and risky in that it produces both harmony and discord. I discern three conditions for the transformation of one static pattern of values into another, whether they are on the same or different levels of reality:

---

[51] Some material for this section is from McManus/2011/244-250.

1 – The 'new' pattern is valued
2 – The 'old' pattern is devalued
3 – The transformation is supported

The first provides the impetus; the second weakens the resistance to change; the third reduces the risk. In the case of a person in transgender, the resistance of families to transition is not only that they do not value the 'new' pattern but that they are part of the 'old' pattern which this person has devalued – not devalued *per se* but only in comparison with something this person perceives as better. However, as people in transition obviously exist socially as well as spiritually/ intellectually, their families' lack of support causes them conflict which only the support of their friends/ faith community/ scholars/ peer support group can overcome.

In the light of my proposed inter-subjective ontology, it can be seen that socio-personal value, though not the only level of existence or wellbeing, is a constituent part of a person's being – without which one faces the experience of annihilation. This is why people in transition, LGB, asexual and intersex people, and other minorities, insist on recognition. Silence, quite literally, equals death.

I became aware of the need for the third condition of this kind of transformation when reading *Phenomenology and Nursing Research*. In his conclusion, Michael Crotty describes sitting in vigil by the bedside of a friend in intensive care, attempting to ignore his preconceptions about nursing and instead letting its experienced reality arise afresh. That reality he names as 'support', following an interview with 'Maureen, a midwife' who states:

> In midwifery, I was thinking, the nurse simply
> supports people while they do what they have to

do and what no one else can do for them. But then it struck me that the nurse is doing very much the same thing in Acute Care too. There too, in the end, you're really supporting people as they do the work of healing themselves. (Crotty/1996/179)[52]

Of course not all bodies do heal themselves. Notwithstanding heroic self-sacrifice for social, intellectual or spiritual reasons – the *biological* superiority of one's life over one's death cannot be denied. Therefore perhaps we may view biological death as a condition brought about by the failure of necessary transformations of elements and simpler biological patterns into the complexity which is a live human body.

This failure then precludes the complex biological patterns necessary to support the sick body as it, quite naturally, strives to attain or regain health. A body immobilised by alcoholic poisoning (sadly, a familiar example in Britain) will strive to eliminate or dilute the poison but if this elimination should block the airway then, lacking oxygen, all systems, such as movement and filtering, vital to support health, will shut down.

Tragically, it can be interference caused by a higher pattern of value which is partly to blame. In this example, many deaths from choking on vomit happen after social occasions, yet it is evident (from our attempts at social control of sexual intercourse and killing) that the social level is morally superior to the biological. This is a clear

---

[52] Original italicised. See all of the "Epilogue: Towards a Phenomenology of Nursing" (Crotty/1996/177-182). Crotty does not acknowledge his source fully (by recording Maureen's surname and the place & date of the interview).

example of Pirsig's (1992/126-127) warning that the levels of static patterns of value are mutually antagonistic.[53]

We have discussed the resulting confusion of morality and should keep this conflict of values in mind as a question as we explore the technology of transformation. From Pirsig's perspective, patterns form because of their constituent values: so to change the values is to change the pattern. Pirsig notes the conflict between Dynamic Quality and static quality, the former which strives to better the *status quo*; and the latter which resists change for better or for worse. And, crucially, he notes that the *status quo* is composed of relationships (as being values being) which are not inexorably determined (*op. cit.*/126-127).

Therefore, transformation occurs when beings, which consistently value other beings, change their tune. When relationships with low probability are revalued, to the detriment of those which had high probability (Jesus's fellowship with women; a man taking female hormones; a comatose body awakening or a healthy one choking to death; people fed to hungry lions for fun) then the patterns of reality change. This change will harmonise with the values of some levels of static quality and will, inevitably, cause dissonance with others. This clash of values means that this change will be perceived simultaneously as moral and immoral/ ethical and unethical.

---

[53] Vomiting is a clear example illustrating the problematic relations of the biological and social levels. See Butler (1999/166-168) on boundaries of the body and polluting persons in Douglas's *Purity and Danger*. See also Hetherington/2000/21: "pollution, while it is often represented in the form of dirt and filth, as is suggested by Mary Douglas' famous definition of dirt as 'matter out of place' is, in fact, a moral category that is expressed in symbolic form."

12 – Hymn of the Upper Room

Shifting, patterns form and reform as fields of fermions seethe, changing state inconstantly, some electrons entangled with others half a universe away, though such descriptions of space make no sense here, on the quantum level. There is no time, only change, in this ludic play of subatomic particles where bosons, the other broad class of particle, wink in and out of existence – some of them photons, from the Greek word for 'light'.

Streaming out from their plasma source in flame, as pools of viscous clear mixed triglyceride esters are transformed into wisps of darker gas, the photons illuminate the larger and smaller conglomerations of compounds on this elementary level of reality. Thirteen large bulks – of mainly hydrogen, oxygen and carbon – extract oxygen from its gassy admixture of, mainly, nitrogen (with smaller amounts of argon) replacing it with carbon dioxide – and occasional methane. These bulks move and, as they do, so do the carbon-compound fibres – such as keratin – covering most of their surface.

The light falls unevenly on the six parallelogram sides of this cuboid of calcite, quartz, feldspar, clay, pyrite and siderite. As well as the bulky bodies, the static structures they recline on, half carbon but sharing elements with the air, cast shadows. Under these structures lie smaller irregular compositions of flat collagen oblong planes, rounded at each end, with straps curving up. On top of these structures are various concave objects of baked kaolin-serpentine, pyrophyllite-talc, mica, vermiculite and smectite and flatter objects with the dull sheen of an alloy of copper and tin. In one is a fermented, flavoured liquid mixture of water and ethanol.

A hand holds a bronze jug and pours wine. On this organic, biological level of reality, the same things can be described differently. Thirteen adult male members of the species *homo sapiens sapiens* are gathered in an elevated den accessed by a stepped passageway leading to the ground. There is some variation in age and size, some more brawny and sunburned than others. Reclining on wooden couches, heads on each other's chests, they drink water and wine and eat lamb, bitter herbs, and unleavened bread – all held in ceramic and bronze dishes on the low wooden table.

The air is warm and the slight breeze through the open windows wafts various aromas around the room. The scent of the smoke arising from the oil lamps, the perfume of the wine and the flavours of the food, the male musk of those portions of their bodies they have not washed recently – and any other bodily odours that may on occasion escape them. The rush matting on the floor, their leather sandals under the couches, the wool of their robes, all these are made of what nowadays we call 'natural fibres'. This description, in that era, would make no sense.

Socially, to move up another level, there is a clear hierarchy in the room (one that will be disrupted, later) with one particular man in charge, the one whose head reclines on the brawny chest of the fisherman named Cephas or Peter, and on whose chest lies the head of a younger man. In this culture, at this time, this exclusive male gathering and physical proximity do not betoken homosexuality but rather cultic celebration and the masculine friendship of free men. The meal proceeds with an easy mixture of formality and relaxation. This is a ritual that is familiar.

The disruptions to the established order are various. A difference between the social patterns of values of church, synagogue or temple and intellectual patterns is that the latter require us to think anew. This is why many followers of Pirsig would categorise religion in general solely as static social quality, to be trumped by intellectual values. Yet, as I have outlined above, Jesus in acting out the role of servant is not only disrupting the social order but also challenging his disciples to accept a new intellectual paradigm: that there is power in service, that domineering might is not always right. In the account in the Fourth Gospel, the Gospel of John, Jesus introduces theological complexities which are now familiar to Christians but at the time must have been intellectually challenging. So challenging, in fact, that some of them may have functioned (and still do) as a *koan*: a maxim intended to stop the mind.

Parting company with Pirsig's stated scheme, but still (I believe) faithful to his inspiration, I posit another level of reality transcending the intellectual, the spiritual. On this level, the words and actions of Jesus that make no sense on any other level find expression. Here too, as on every level, the objects, expressions and actions on other levels are revalued. So the ludic fermions and bosons composing the mixed triglyceride esters, that on the biological level are no more than olive oil, serving socially only to illuminate the gathering, barely registering on the intellectual level, are on the spiritual level reminders of the parable of preparation (the 'wise and foolish virgins' waiting for the bridegroom), of all the references to healing and ease and gladness betokened by oil in the Hebrew scriptures – and, to contrast heuristics with hermeneutics –

of the ancient olive trees, lifeblood of families, cut down by occupying forces in Palestine today.

So when Jesus, in Aramaic, speaks the words, '*den bisri*', in Greek, '*soma mu*', in Latin, '*corpus meum*', in English, 'my body', that reality, that sign, has already multiple levels of signification.

My conclusion when I wrote on the acrimonious, theological, political and extremely personal debate over abortion (I don't pick easy subjects!) is that there is so much disagreement over the termination of life in a woman's womb because there is no agreement on the nature of that life. In other words, we will never agree on abortion until we agree on pregnancy.

Similarly, churches cannot agree on the nature of the bread and wine changed by the presence of the body of Christ until they agree on the nature of that body. Feminists cannot agree on the nature of transgendered bodies until they agree on the nature of gendered bodies (and with more and more and more theory, that discussion is *far* from over). We are using the same words for very different things indeed. A mathematician friend of mine scoffed when I used the phrase, 'different levels of reality', as if there were only one. I hope I have shown that there are many. We may argue about their categorisation and nomenclature (organic chemistry can hardly be called 'inorganic' I admit but it's not clear to me that it's biological) but not that they exist.

So, *from a spiritual and socio-personal perspective*, there is a shift in reality when Jesus picks up the bread and cup of wine and says 'this is my body; this is my blood'. He, the priest or minister, we, revalue those elements, devaluing their elemental and biological status in favour of a transfiguration that at once returns them to the ludic play of luminous unpatterned reality and to the mystical miracle of the divine community where Love, loving Love, is encountered in communion.

In a secular view, there is still the possibility of using this empowering perspective of value and revaluing as basic to the composition of our universe – and so also fundamental to our understanding of our very bodies and of our very selves. It is important, therefore, to realise that in the Pirsigian metaphysics which I present here there is can be no division of fact and value. This statement, heretical to modern ears, has its philosophical justification in a venerable tradition in which the question of the relation between appearance and reality has led the dialectical debate – one which the next chapter summarises.

13 – Reality as value, in harmony and conflict

The absolute mathematical view of reality that most scientists take for granted and which Pirsig names as 'classical' or 'theoretical', has a classical root predating Plato's *Protagoras*, as James L. Jarret explains:[54]

> For Paramenides and his school (most notably Zeno of Elea, the inventor of such famous paradoxes as the denial of movement, for in order to move, anything would have to move either in its place or in a place where it is not – neither of which makes sense) the difficulties which attend the acceptance of change led them to the severe position of regarding the whole sensory world as illusory, since the senses manifestly report change. Plato was greatly influenced by this philosophy (Jarret/1969/10)

A pupil of Zeno, Leucippus of Miletus, moved to Abdera and there taught Democritus and it is from this Thracian soil and from this latter 'contemporary of Socrates' (Jarret/1969) that the other classical root of theoretical reality grows:

> He is generally accepted as the founder of atomism, and to have coined the term "atom" for the smallest possible particle, literally the "uncuttable". (Jarret/1969/10)

> Democritus was not at all frightened away by the strangeness of attributing existence to nothing:

---

[54] See McManus/2011/90-100. If you are neither a philosopher nor a theologian (or even if you are) and you skim or even skip this chapter, I'll never know – but do read the last page and think about it. Especially the next time you're tempted to devalue someone!

[...] Parmenides is right in saying that without blank space, there can be no movement, but where he was wrong was in concluding that therefore movement is impossible. Of course things move; look at them. Therefore void exists. (Jarret/1969/11)[55]

These 'pre-Socratic' proclamations may seem rather removed from our modern problematic relationship to technology, our 'value-free' perspective on reality and hazy definitions of Quality; yet the subsequent move of Democritus provides a link, which Stephen Menn then explains:

Sweet exists by convention, bitter by convention, colour by convention; atoms and Void (alone) exist in reality.... We know nothing accurately in reality, but (only) as it changes according to the bodily condition, and the constitution of those things that flow upon (the body) and impinge upon us. (Democritus)[56]

The fifth Meditation does not explicitly say that only geometrical truths can be distinctively conceived in material things, or that they constitute the whole essence of bodies, but Descartes thinks he is entitled to this conclusion, and he draws it explicitly at *Principles of*

---

[55] Emphasis original. Jarret here seems to be both paraphrasing and agreeing with the argument of Democritus *contra* Paramenides.
[56] Jarret does not state if the ellipsis is original to Democritus or Freeman, and he references thus: Democritus, in Kathleen Freeman, *Ancilla to the Pre-Socratic Philosophers* (Cambridge: Harvard University Press, 1957), p. 104, No. 125. I conflate reference information from: Jarret/1969/6,11,12.

Philosophy II: 4, entitled "that the nature of body consists not in weight, hardness, color, or the like, but in extension alone." Descartes' evidence here is not simply his inability to discover distinct ideas of sensible qualities, but his positive ability to form a distinct conception of an extension existing by itself without any superadded qualities. (Menn/1998/358)

In the latter quote, Menn translates Descartes' *'accidenta'*[57] as 'qualities', as is traditional and perfectly correct; *accidenta* may also be translated as 'attributes', which does not have the connotation of qualification as modification and, interestingly in Pirsigian terms, can mean: that composition of an object which is gifted by a subject. 'Quality' and 'qualities' are confusable terms in English, in that their linguistic relation of singular and plural may lead to the erroneous reading of a similar relation in the Greek philosophical terms they translate.

Translators and the English language are not to blame if the eye of the reader skips from 'quality' to 'qualities' without perceiving the profound difference in concept. Both Plato and Aristotle employ a variety of terms for both – however they do not confuse the two.[58]

This exposition serves to demonstrate that the tradition which Pirsig is challenging is ancient and though both Democritus and Descartes may have been superseded as philosophers, their influence, on the way we conceive

---

[57] Latin. See Menn/1998/356-366 for discussion on Descartes' position on 'accidents' and quantity.

[58] I draw out these linguistic points to explain why, throughout this book, and in my thesis, I do not confuse the terms 'quality' and 'qualities' but use the former only as equivalent to 'virtue' and the latter only as equivalent to *'accidenta'*.

reality, continues. The view of the primacy of quantification which Pirsig (1999/74) describes as the 'death force' has such an inescapable stranglehold on ethics precisely because it claims to be identical with reality in its purest and truest form, as we have seen:

a distinct conception of an extension existing by itself without any superadded qualities. (Menn/1998/358)

Having explored the roots of Pirsig's 'Classical' or 'theoretical' component of reality, we can now perceive his juxtaposed 'Romantic' or 'esthetic' component in its philosophical context. Pirsig's philosophical perspective can seem confusing on this point, as he appears to identify these 'superadded qualities' sometimes with the Romantic/esthetic quality and sometimes with Quality itself. He uses an analogy of a train for knowledge and has 'Classic Knowledge' as 'the engine and all the boxcars' and 'Romantic Quality' as 'the leading edge of the engine' where 'there are no subjects, no objects, only the track of Quality ahead'.[59]

Perhaps an American readership will understand the arrival of the train, a stock image in the frontier imaginary, as the shock of the new – which can refer to Quality. There are obvious profound postcolonial objections. However, although this image may be (as is Pirsig himself) Midwestern in origin, a confused meaning can only arise if we do not distinguish between its metaphysical and epistemological meaning. The train is, as he states, a train of *knowledge*. To understand this apparent contradiction, we must, briefly, review the context in which it occurs. Pirsig develops his metaphysics from his mentor F.S.C.

---

[59] All quotes and paraphrase Pirsig/1999/282-283

Northrop, who discusses (in his chapter on the United States) the thought of Descartes, Newton and John Locke:

> Descartes's physics had a very short life and was rejected following the publication of Newton's *Principia*. The Anglo-American philosophy of Newton's physics is that of John Locke. (Northrop/1946/72)

Northrop points out that there are:

> inescapable difficulties to which the facts of the physics of Galilei and Newton gave rise when it distinguished between sensed data in sensed space and public, physical objects in mathematically defined space, and thereby gave rise to the problem concerning the relation between the two, for which John Locke's philosophy is the first, and, as it turns out, a self-contradictory answer. (Northrop/1946/72)

However E.A Burtt, in his chapter 'Criticism of Newton's Philosophy of Space and Time' takes issue with Newton's attempt to sort out Descartes' confusion on absolute measurement 'with an ingenious use of language' (Burtt/1999/262):

> absolute time and space as thus understood, by their own nature negate the possibility that sensible bodies can move *with reference* to them – such bodies can only move *in* them, *with reference to other bodies*. Why is this so? Simply because they are infinite and homogenous entities; one part of them is quite indistinguishable from any other equal part; any position in them is identical with any position;

for wherever that part or position may be it is surrounded by an infinite stretch of similar room in all directions. (Burtt/1999/256)

Northrop (1946/111-16) explains John Locke's triple metaphysical relation – physical substances; mental substances (observer); and sense data ('aesthetic continuum') – and how the nominalist Bishop Berkeley proved Locke's material substance meaningless, as David Hume proved mental substance (observer) meaningless also. Northrop is left with the 'aesthetic component' and the 'theoretic component'.[60] Mary Midgley, in *Science as Salvation: A Modern Myth and its Meaning*, provides a caveat:

the unobserved world did not really exist except as a set of ideas in the mind of God. Berkeley was an 'idealist' in the full metaphysical sense [...] Berkeley's ideas, however, have been taken up by theorists who did not always notice what drastic changes they called for.

Nineteenth-century thinkers, following Ernst Mach, adopted this notion as a general explanation of scientific claims about the external world [...] instrumentalism was transplanted without the soil in which it had originally grown (Midgley/1992/122)

If this is true for Berkeley then it is also true for Kant, who held the (mentally) sensed, empirical, aesthetic continuum to be *a posteriori* to the imagined, ideal, *a priori* theoretical component; he held the former to be contingent and the latter necessary. Northrop disagrees: the

---

[60] Northrop/1946/441-454

theoretical, the humble basis of the scientific method, is hypothetical and subject to revolution caused by new empirical evidence; the aesthetic is just as primary and while ephemeral, is nonetheless immediate and real. It is on the basis of this insight of Northrop that Pirsig can state:

> Reality is always the moment of vision *before* the intellectualization takes place. *There is no other reality.* This preintellectual reality is what Phaedrus felt he had properly identified as Quality. (Pirsig/1999/247)

Pirsig here seems to be blurring the distinction between his concept of Quality and romantic quality.[61] This distinction can be maintained only if Pirsig is speaking here of an epistemological and not a metaphysical reality. However, in my reading Pirsig's work, this quoted text can be clarified: the 'pre-intellectual' vision is the apprehension of the patterns of value, the web of relationships which constitutes reality. Pirsig uses the word 'relationship' if not in definition at least in situation:

> Quality couldn't be independently related with either the subject or the object but could be found *only in the relationship of the two with each other*…The Quality event is the cause of the subjects and objects[62]

This relationship is one of harmony. There are grave metaphysical consequences if this step is not taken. If Quality is left as 'event' or even situated in 'relationship'

---

[61] Pirsig here seems to follow Northrop's confusion of undifferentiated and differentiated aesthetic components.

[62] Pirsig/1999/239, italics in original.

then it could be read as 'value-neutral'. Pirsig is clearly against this concept:

> There's a principle in physics that if a thing can't be distinguished from anything else it doesn't exist. To this the Metaphysics of Quality adds a second principle: if a thing has no value it isn't distinguished from anything else. Then, putting the two together, *a thing that has no value does not exist.*[63]

Pirsig takes seriously Cartesian/ Augustinian scepticism: but, unlike them, grounds his epistemology only in experience and does not take faith in divinity as his starting point. Augustine and Descartes start with God and finish with a value-free, inert, mechanical universe. For Pirsig, value is the basis of reality and integral to the cosmos, as is value conflict. This is important because, in this metaphysics, an attack on someone's value is an attack on their very being.

The next chapter explores ideological conflict and offers a possible truce.

---

[63] Pirsig/1992/121, italics original.

14 – Competing truths & strategic truce

Masculum et Feminam is the title of a booklet I wrote for an education campaign in Scotland. The subtitle is *Time for Inclusive Education and the Conservative Catholic*.[64] The Latin is taken from the 27th verse in the first chapter of the first book of the Bible, Genesis:

> *Et creavit Deus hominem ad imaginem suam;*
> *ad imaginem Dei creavit illum,*
> *masculum et feminam creavit eos.*

The Jerusalem Bible translates this verse as:

> God created man in the image of himself,
> in the image of God he created him,
> male and female he created them.

The Latin is, perhaps surprisingly, a more exact and inclusive translation than the English as it does not insert gender-specific Divine pronouns which are not present in the original Hebrew. And, as the word '*hominem*' can mean 'human' as well as 'man', so '*illum*' can be used as a generic human object pronoun. In fairness, the word 'man' was used similarly in English until recently. A more up-to-date translation would be:

> God created humans in the image of God,
> in the image of God they were created,
> male and female God created them.

This is the foundational verse that informs conservative Christian teaching on gender. Interestingly, a traditionally reflective method used by many Jewish scholars (who best understand Hebrew) can read this verse as an affirmation of the Divine image in each human – and as the Bible

---

[64] McManus/2016, this section is largely taken from this booklet.

expresses the Hebrew understanding of God in male and female and non-gender-specific terms, so too may each human person, made in God's image, be similarly understood. Indeed a Biblical writer usually (mis)quoted in conservative Christian attacks on LGBT people, proclaims:

> and there are no more distinctions between Jew
> and Greek, slave and free, male and female, but
> all of you are one in Christ Jesus.
> (Galatians 3:28)

The letters of St Paul were written in Greek and the original language of the verse is very emphatic.[65] The above translation from the Jerusalem Bible has the added word 'distinctions' (from the sense of the chapter) but this is not actually what is written. The original says this:

> There is no Jew or Greek, there is no slave or
> free, there is no male or female, for all of you are
> one in Christ Jesus. (Galatians 3:28)

However, my booklet was written with conservative lay Catholics in mind and they tend not to be very interested in translations or interpretations of Scripture as the Bible was read in Catholics churches in Latin until very recently, and usually not read in Catholic households at all. What they *are* interested in, however, is the teaching of the Church,

---

[65] The language of 'grafting' onto the rootstock of Judaism, 'the cultivated olive', the new growth of the Christian community as a 'wild olive' – which St Paul (Romans 11:24) describes as 'beyond nature' παρὰ φύσιν (*para phusin*) – may also be applicable to life-enhancing surgery, including gender transition. For discussion on the same term used pejoratively in Romans 1:26-27, see McManus/2013/Ch.3.

especially that of the teaching body called the *Magisterium* and principally that of the pope.[66]

Pope Francis, ironically, is receiving a lot of criticism from conservative Catholics for his teaching recently promulgated in an encyclical entitled, *The Joy of Love*, which has a rather startling paragraph on gender:

> Nor can we ignore the fact that the configuration of our own mode of being, whether as male or female, is not simply the result of biological or genetic factors, but of multiple elements having to do with temperament, family history, culture, experience, education, the influence of friends, family members and respected persons, as well as other formative situations. It is true that we cannot separate the masculine and the feminine from God's work of creation, which is prior to all our decisions and experiences, and where biological elements exist which are impossible to ignore. But it is also true that masculinity and femininity are not rigid categories.
> (*Amoris Laetitia*, paragraph 286)

There is even the possibility, in *Amoris Laetitia* paragraph 56, for a positive appraisal of LGBT families:[67] There is no stereotype of the ideal family but a mosaic of many different realities with all their joys, hopes and

---

[66] Until the Second Vatican Council ending in 1965; which is also when this verse was definitively applied to slavery. St Paul was most interested in the division between Jew and gentile (non-Jew), so it's taken about 2,000 years for the inspired and revolutionary message of this verse to be extended from the first clause to the second. We may not have to wait that long until it is applied to gender too.
[67] What follows is my paraphrase.

problems – the situations that concern us are challenges calling for a revival of hope, the source of prophetic visions, transformative actions and creative forms of charity.

So, although strong opposition to transgender has come from conservative Christians, there are both Biblical and Magisterial views which are more open to positive interpretation. Many conservative Christians are either adherents of the doctrine of *sola scriptura* (that only scripture is a sure guide to salvation) or at least nominally obedient to the authority of the *Magisterium*. Of the others, many are either Orthodox or Anglican.

I am quite aware that most Orthodox churches do not have the same relationship to the *Magisterium* as those under the authority of the Pope, however there is a mutual respect for the interpretation of tradition – and many conservative High Anglicans are famously 'more Roman than Rome', therefore these are still useful resources when in discussion with them.

With that reminder of fruitful crosspollination in discussion, let's revisit the beginning of this book in order to consider what has been suggested as an aid to resolution in each debate and to remind ourselves of the difference between them:

What these two debates have in common is that on one side of each there is an assertion of a reality inaccessible to, and independent of, the evidence of the five human senses; on the other side of each there is an assertion of the distinction between symbol, similarity and identity.

The difference lies in the nature of the assertion. Catholics who believe in transubstantiation (that bread and wine become only body and blood) use the mediaeval language of scholasticism to explain their belief in this mystical change and presence. In contrast, transactivists do not put forward their assertion (that a man can undergo a transition and become a woman, retroactively, or vice-versa*) as a belief but as a fact that must be accepted irrespective of any lack of medical evidence and irreducible to personal psychology.*

Whereas Catholics consider those who do not accept their assertion to be lacking in faith, but not necessarily in goodwill or intelligence, transactivists accuse their doubters of transphobia and while respecting their right to free speech, deny them a platform to exercise it.

Some directive questions, rather than definitive answers, may, with patient reflection and the benefit of lived experience, point towards at least some harmonious resolution of each debate:

What would be gained, in terms of Christology, ecclesiology and ecumenical relations if a Pirsigian metaphysical paradigm and Pythagorean mystical metaphor of music replaced the Aristotelian paradigm of substance and accidents and the change and presence signalling the encounter of believer and Redeemer in the Eucharist was understood (inasmuch as mystery can ever be comprehended) as transposition of the elements into the New Song that is Christ?

The one reality which Second and Third Wave feminists agree on is the need for resistance to oppression of women and minorities. Donna Harroway's post-structuralist 'A Cyborg Manifesto', references Chela Sandoval in defining 'oppositional consciousness' as a 'model of political identity' being 'about contradictory locations and heterochronic calendars, not about relativisms and pluralisms' (Haraway/1993/320).

What would be gained, in terms of such a strategic alliance, by a truce between feminists and transactivists, on the following three conditions?

1 – no policing of gender performance
2 – admittance to women-only space of transsexual women but not of transvestite men
3 – inclusion on public platforms of critical scholarship on transgender issues that is respectful to the lived experience of people in transition

The next chapter introduces the difficult topic of identity – and the production and reception of its performance.

15 – Identity and performance

One mellow evening in the beautiful Andalusian city of Granada, my tranquil dinner with good Spanish friends was interrupted by loud offbeat drumming. My friends are child psychologists and they were talking about the danger of saying (*e.g.* of a little girl) that, 'she does that because she's autistic' rather than realising that 'she does that and the term "autistic" is helpful in describing her behaviour'. It was an interesting discussion, and related to ideas of nominalism, so I was not happy at the interruption.

The drummer was a Northern European White 'hippy', the term the locals use for the inhabitants of the caves on the Sacromonte, who are often makers and hawkers of jewellery, often recipients of Spanish social security (while disparaging of paid work and professing to be outside of 'the system') and whose dwellings usually do not have the benefits of showers – making their inhabitants rather pungent in the heat. In comparison to the Gypsy flamenco guitarists, violinists and drummers native to the city, their musical skills were usually judged as inferior.[68]

Seated at tables outside the restaurant (Granada has excellent *tapas*, even for vegetarians) we were a captive audience and, at the end of the forced recital, the musician shook her dreadlocks in anger at the lack of applause, complained loudly – in fairly good Spanish – picked up her bongo drums and stomped off. Dinner resumed. Conflict of opinion is not considered a huge problem in Granada.

Even the title of Susan Bennett's *Theatre Audiences: A Theory of Production and Reception* (1997) makes clear

---

[68] For a far more positive appraisal of 'hippies' and other '*okupas*', see my ethnographic dissertation: *Dreaming Anarchy: a Shut-Eye View of a Utopia* (McManus/2015a).

that performance does not depend totally on the performer. In order to be successful, it has to be well-received.

My first objection to the notion that reality is socially constructed is that it is speciesist; my second objection is of categorical confusion – specifically that of epistemology (discourse of knowledge) with ontology (discourse of being). Another episode of – successful – performance may illustrate this.

In Season 2 of the modern American televised melodrama *Desperate Housewives*,[69] the story arc for Lynette Scavo and her husband Tom focuses on their gender role conflicts in terms of professional work and childcare. Basically she's the better breadwinner, and it makes more sense if he takes over as homemaker.

The episode happens at work, where Lynette (played by Felicity Huffman) is a heterosexual female advertising executive required to take over the online titillation of her male boss's wife by text. In theatrical terms, this is an example of what playwright and director Bertold Brecht named *Verfremdungseffekt* (distancing/ alienation) – as the audience is invited to laugh at the success of the textual titillation rather than be aroused by it. So one aspect of this episode is that the carnality associated with this practice is problematised by its setting in the realm of the imagination.

There are several instances of *Verfremdungseffekt* here, as the narratives are 'nested' inside each other like Russian dolls. There are the instant messenger texts composing the conversation seen on a computer screen; there is the conversation of 'Lynette' and her 'co-workers' about the

---

[69] Episode 20, 'It Wasn't Meant to Happen', written by Marc Cherry & Tom Spezialy, directed by Larry Shaw, aired on ABC TV (USA) on 30th April 2006.

conversation which includes hypotheses – which the audience are obviously meant to share – about what the unseen woman is doing; there is the setting of the workplace; there is Lynette's relationship of employee (and subordinate) to her boss and of wife (and equal) to her husband; there is Lynette's performed heterosexuality and female sex and gender of non-trans woman; there is the presence (unseen by the TV audience but not perhaps by the studio audience) of the camera crew and other production crew; there is the TV or computer screen of each audience individual or group; there is the physical location of each audience; there are the work and romantic contexts of each member of the audience; there are wider social contexts (local, national, global).

The gag, in this performance, is that it's successful. 'Lynette' (a heterosexual female/ woman) is pretending to be something that she's not (a heterosexual male/ man) and is getting away with it. It's funny, if you like that kind of obvious humour, and there is no explicit link with the gendered story arc. Felicity Huffman had previously starred in *Transamerica* (2005)[70] as a male to female transsexual, again pretending to be something that she's not.

Or was she? The social construction of reality notion leaves no appeal to objective identity. Butler would see each and every identity in all these nested narratives as performed and insubstantial. Crucially, she would also see them as temporary. To the unseen woman supposedly receiving these texts, the sender is her husband and in that narrative 'Lynette' successfully performs his role. Yet can we accept that she *really* is her boss, even temporarily?

---

[70] Written & directed by Duncan Tucker, released by IFC Films & The Western Company.

If we can, and this is the claim of Queer theory at base, then there can be no accusations of 'misgendering': someone's gender identity (or any other identity) is only as valid as their temporary performance of it. If any of the individuals or groups of audience members who compose the social reception of that performance find fault in it, they are perfectly able to dismiss it as unsuccessful.

Is this where we wish to leave ontology? Identity dependent on ratings? In an attempt to free them from imposed socially-assigned gender-roles, critical theorists have transformed autonomous individuals into performers vulnerable to ephemeral 'feels'.[71]

The notion of socially-constructed reality has led to other categorical confusion, two infamous recent cases being that of 'transracial' Rachel Dolezal and the far more complex case of 'JT LeRoy', also known as Laura Albert.

In an interview titled 'The Heart of Whiteness', Ijeoma Oluo appears to really try to understand the motivation for Dolezal's performance but cannot accept that 'racial fluidity is anything more than a function of her privilege as a white person'. Oluo (2017) also rejects her appeal to the social construction of race:

> "Race is just a social construct" is a retort I get quite often from white people who don't want to talk about black issues anymore. A lot of things in our society are social constructs – money, for example – but the impact they have on our lives, and the rules by which they operate, are very real. I cannot undo the evils of capitalism simply by pretending to be a millionaire. (Oluo/2017)

---

[71] 'Feels' refers to audience reaction. See, for example, 'Teens React to Slender' (2012) on *The Fine Brothers on You Tube*.

Rachel Dolezal has changed her name to Nkechi Amare Diallo and asserts: 'some people will forever see me as my birth category, as a white woman. But people who see me as that don't see me really for who I am' (*ibid*). She sees herself as 'a light-skinned black woman' (*ibid*).

In contrast, Laura Albert (also known, on occasion, as 'Emily Frasier') does not feel that she has been misidentified but rather that her successful performance of an individual of different age, sex, gender, health, accent, occupation, ethnicity and place of birth was an authentic act of creativity.

> The lively documentary *Author: The JT LeRoy Story* purports to explain and defend the phenomenon that was "Jeremiah 'Terminator' LeRoy," the socially-phobic, southern-accented, homeless, transgender (male-born), HIV-positive teenage prostitute and transgressive novelist who turned out to be a fat Jewish 30-something woman from Brooklyn. (Edelstein/2016)[72]

The objective reality of gender identity claims are not only complicated by Queer theory's rejection of ontology but by the phenomena of desisting and detransitioning. The BBC 2 documentary *Transgender Kids: Who Knows Best?* (12th Jan. 2017) was criticised for including segments referring to Dr Kenneth Zucher:

> a Toronto child psychologist who was removed from his post as head of the city's gender clinic for failing to toe the affirmative line, essentially

---

[72] David Edelstein adds: 'I use the adjective fat advisedly, because that's the word Laura Albert – the woman who was JT but pretended to be "Speedie," JT's British confidante – repeats in the lengthy interview that shapes the movie.' (Edelstein/2016).

by arguing that gender dysphoria is something that can be influenced by any number of mental health factors. [...] Also explored were a range of links between gender dysphoria, autism and suicide, and the question of whether transitioning is always the right answer.

Jeffreys, similarly criticised as transphobic, begins her conclusion, 'The Abolition of Gender', by justifying her opposition to gender transition as an expression not of solidarity not only with women but with anyone hurt by the gender binary:

> The 'gender belief' system, that is the idea that there are essential differences between women and men, forms the justification and sorting system for women's subordination. This book is focussed on one problematic product of this system in the present, transgenderism, and sought to show its harms, and it has argued that 'gender', as it is encapsulated in transgenderism, hurts many. (Jeffreys/2014/181)

A discourse that dismisses gender transition on grounds of its impossibility, and simultaneously affirms a traditional binary construction of gender, is very different from a discourse that seeks to abolish the gender binary as fraudulent and oppressive – and therefore sees gender transition as a hurtful move from one oppressive location to another (a definition transactivists resist). Admittedly, while adherents of the former may be clear about its lack of compassion for the lived experience of people making that transition, adherents of the latter discourse may come across as so angry about ideological false consciousness that people in transition absolutely fail to feel their love!

As someone who has had heterosexual, homosexual and transsexual relationships, I can at times be very dismissive of the categories of sexual attraction (and of the assumption that all of us experience it) but I cannot deny the lived experience of the men who have been beaten up because some other man was homophobic. So while I sympathise a great deal with calls for the abolition of gender (and of race, and of class)[73] as these classifications quite obviously do us humans great harm, I cannot fail to be present to reality as people now experience it in their daily lives – and understand that, for example, the masculine identity which I take for granted may be the long-cherished dream of someone identified as female at birth.

So too, while I may personally resist the sign 'bisexual', I cannot be insensitive to the huge personal affirmation of agency that coming out as gay may mean for another man. And, although I personally have no wish to live as a woman, I acknowledge that the fight for those identified as male at birth who do is far from easy – and may not be made easier if I trash the whole project from the lofty tower of Academe.[74]

Oluo (2017) makes the point that 'racial fluidity' is a 'one-way street', that 'claims of blackness' (such as Dolezal's) do nothing 'to open up the definition of

---

[73] See the exhilarating (but very disturbing) call of xenofeminists to abolish gender, race and class – and to attempt the first primarily through the provision of DIY hormonal engineering! www.laboriacuboniks.net (in various European languages but with flashing images).

[74] I don't believe that this is what Jeffreys is attempting to do, although I do know that many people in gender transition are very hurt and angered by her words.

whiteness to those with darker skin, coarser hair, or racialized features' (*ibid*) and that the 'history of "passing" in the United States is a story filled with pain and separation. It has never been a story of liberation' (*ibid*).

So, is it possible to open up the categories of gender – while we work for their abolition? A transsexual friend, who wishes to remain anonymous, told me some years ago that he felt that young people were less inclined to seek hormonal and surgical transition than when he had and were instead simply performing their preferred gender in their preferred way. I'm not sure if that observation is statistically still true but, as a playwright and dramaturg, I am very interested in the possibilities of performance.

My observation of sensational performance of identity, such as that of Rachel Dolezal/ Nkechi Amare Diallo, Laura Albert/ JT LeRoy – and even of the celebrated fake Anna Anderson/ surviving Romanov Princess Anastasia – is that the ingenuity and artistry of the performance is matched by the level of outrage when people discover that the individuals are not who they say they are (or whom others have assumed them to be). It seems that we still have some sense of reality that is not simply that of an individual assertion, however artistically or politically performed.

I have said that as gender theorists repudiate the possibility of any meaningful objective discourse to describe reality, then their assertion of either natural or intentional gender ·identity (or any identity at all) is meaningless. However, with the insight that reality is multilayered and an inter-subjective experience of patterns of values, and so the social level is no less real than the biological, there is some scope for a fuller answer.

The performance of masculinity by 'Lynette' was aided by the medium of a computer screen. As many modern-day users of dating apps have found out (and as many have not!) there is absolutely no necessary relationship between someone's online persona and their presence 'in the flesh'. Similarly, Laura Albert was able to construct 'JT LeRoy' as a semi-autobiographical author with few logistical difficulties in that performance – until the public demanded to meet him. As recounted by *The Guardian* journalist Steve Rose (2016) she then had the problem of casting Savannah Knoop (her boyfriend's half-sister) and directing her to stand in as his body double. With the twist that this double was both single and original. Such was the celebrity hype surrounding this character that she was even able to direct this non-transgender female to convince another famous director, also a non-transgender female, that she was a male to female transsexual. Even when they were naked. The duped director's subsequent response was: 'I'm a fool. How could I not see it?' (*ibid*).

Rachel Dolezal, on the other hand, was in the flesh from the start of her performance as Black. Which necessitated make-up and was accessorised with box braids. I have no idea if this performance was continued in bed – or how she managed to secure a position as a professor of Black History with degrees in Art rather than History (Oluo/2017).

What I'm interested in is how all of these performances utilised various props, costumes, stagings, lines, direction, and, yes, lighting (*ibid*)[75] to achieve a positive reception – however temporary. When we broaden our awareness of reality, we can allow contradictions on various levels. So,

---

[75] Dolezal complains that Oluo is making her sit in full lighting to be photographed so that she looks White.

although it is quite obvious that, for someone to perform as a man, possession of a penis is quite handy, this biological prop need not be a prerequisite for a successful performance. It would be unthinkable to inform a man who had his penis severed in an accident that, simply for that reason, he was no longer a man. Similarly, who would have the cruelty to rule that a woman suffering from breast or ovarian cancer and forced only for that reason to have a mastectomy or hysterectomy was therefore no longer a woman?

Biology, in that sense, is clearly not identity. As for chromosomes, appealing to them as an ultimate reference for binary gender reality is a form of reductionism typical of those who only trust empirical evidence. What these people fail to understand is that empirical evidence only presents *itself* (and even that statement needs the qualification of the huge debates over competing rationales for theories and methods of data collection and analysis). The evolution of science does not proceed by testing but by the creation of hypotheses in the hope that we may find a more harmonious fit for the data. There is always another hypothesis and data collection cannot prove any of them, only offer qualified support (Pirsig/1999/259-270).

In any case, why stop with chromosomes? Ultimate reality cannot be the preserve of either biology or even chemistry – not when the magical quantum universe underlies and undermines all attempts at ultimately defining patterns. In reality, all experience of patterns of value is real. Even when the performance is a fiction. To revisit the musical metaphor I have used above, the composition of a pattern of values may be understood as the performance of a musical chord – necessitating the inclusion of notes in harmony and the exclusion of dissonant notes which would break the pattern. But are dissonant notes cleverly played around harmonious ones not the basis of jazz?

It has to be admitted that there are, however, unsuccessful performances of identity, including gender. Some years ago, the university LGBT society of which I was a member had a huge online and in person controversy which flared up when one of the young men was thrown out for making slighting reference to the lack of male genitalia of a young person wishing to join men's events (we also had women's events, trans events and events for all). This person, who most of the time presented as female, on occasion simply put her long hair up under a *bunnet* (as we say in Scotland, woollen cap or beanie elsewhere) and assumed a male name.

Some years later I heard that she now had resolved to live as female (which everyone I knew accepted as her identified gender at birth) and many people – who had found the performance extremely annoying and attention-seeking – found in this proof that all the time she was a fake.

I can sympathise with these sentiments, although, personally, I found her friendly and refreshingly free of the ageism to which the young gay men especially were prone. I can also say that she brought up a topic that had never been dealt with in the Society and greater accommodation was made than had been before. So perhaps I am too judgemental when I say that her transgender performance was not a success. Performance, like identity, is a many-splendored thing.

The next chapter takes up a particular issue of signs and identity – the territorial polemic of toilets.

16 – The trouble with toilets

An intrinsic part of Pirsig's metaphysical hierarchy of static quality is the conflictual nature of the various levels. Although I rename and add to his hierarchy, I retain this concept of moral conflict and it is this aspect which may explain the current moral panic over transgender toilets. To those adamantly opposed/in support the issue is one of self-evident right/wrong: transgender people have the/no human right to access toilets of their preferred gender – rather than that identified at birth.

Why? What is it about toilets that brings out such ire? I quoted (above) the famous definition by Mary Douglas of dirt as 'matter out of place'. Toilets are where dirt, human dirt, is put in its place. Urine, faeces, sweat, blood, vomit, sperm, menses, snot, puss, phlegm, hair, nails, scabs, saliva, sebum, sputum, skin, wax, tears, all these human *excretae* may end up down the toilet or the plughole. It is the ultimate insult to kill someone on the toilet or throw a body into a cesspit.

Yet, to misquote the mediaeval philosopher Aquinas (speaking of female prostitution) the toilet is the sewer that keeps us clean.[76] So why is it not considered the most moral of places? In Pirsig's scheme a toilet is the *locus* of the conflict between social and biological static quality; it is also the place where biological functions are regulated so that social values are undisturbed.

Under this definition (which is my paraphrase of Pirsig's thought) the kitchen, the garden, the bedroom and the

---

[76] *Opera Omnia* Vol. XVI *Opuscula Theologica et Philosophica*. In the view of this Doctor of the Church, it's the only defence against sodomy! St. Thomas was influenced by the equally infamous and similar statement of Augustine of Hippo in *De Ordine* II. 4 (12).

diningroom all share in this conflicted location. So it appears that the only places in the house which are not conflicted in this manner are the cupboard under the stairs and the front parlour – unless one is either sneezing, playing Sardines or having high tea!

Perhaps the toilet gets such bad press because, unlike the other domestic locations mentioned, the biological functions which it regulates are usually personal rather than social – and because they involve excretion not ingestion there is the instinctual feeling of aversion. Perhaps I am over-scrupulous but I would far rather witness someone taking even the nastiest medicine than I would put up with them parading about from room to room brushing their teeth. I admit this may be a minority view.

Extending this view of the social and the personal, there is a distinct difference in atmosphere in male and female toilets. In the former, where there are a row of urinals or a urinal wall, persons with a penis walk in and without more ado manually extract it from their underwear and stick it out – in public view – in order to aim the stream of urine. Eye contact in this location is generally considered a biological signal of either sex or violence. Washing and drying hands (if it occurs at all!) is brief, functional and suspicious if extended. In the latter, persons with a vagina wait for a cubicle to be free, enter it (alone or with a close friend) and close the door, then come out and spend some time at the sink and mirror where social eye contact is as expected as washing and drying hands, and conversation naturally occurs.

Therefore, for a person with a penis to introduce themselves into a female toilet is to risk being perceived as a threat if they did not signal female friendliness. A person with a vagina in a male toilet would risk the same unless they also avoided making social signs that in this location would be interpreted as either seduction or aggression. I feel (perhaps I am old-fashioned) that it is in no way sexist to suggest that, in both of these scenarios, persons with a vagina are more vulnerable to persons with a penis than *vice-versa*.

So, is it that simple? Rather than have toilets for 'Men' and 'Women' (or Ladies and Gentlemen) shall we instead have toilets for persons with a vagina and persons with a penis? What about intersex people? Transvestites? Survivors of penile rape? Religious people? Shy people? Sex workers? Accompanied minors of another gender? Homosexuals?

Nowhere in his two *roman-a-thèse* philosophical novels does Pirsig address these precise situations, but in the central chapter of *Lila*, his second novel, he has intriguing observations on the eponymous character and the distinction between her biological patterns of value (that are attracted to his fit male body) and her social patterns of value (that despise him as a 'sad sack'). After an unresolved argument, they make silent love in the dark and he finds old scars on her wrist:

> The mental Lila had tried to die but the cellular Lila had wanted to live.
>
> That's the way it always is. The intelligence of the mind can't think of any reason to live, but it goes on anyway because the intelligence of the cells can't think of any reason to die.
>
> That explained what had happened tonight. The first intelligence out there in the cabin disliked him and still did. It was this second intelligence

that had come in and made love. The first Lila
had nothing to do with it. (Pirsig/1992/234-235)

The point is that social and biological levels of reality
have very little to do with each other. The problem is that
female toilets are locations for both whereas male toilets
are solely for the latter. Generally speaking. So this
complicates the easy assignation of biological function to
biological location. A further complication is that both
locations are highly territorial – and that female toilets
have an added element of solidarity as they are considered
sanctuary from marauding males.

One solution may be to allow persons with a penis,
irrespective of their social expression of gender, to use a
toilet containing both urinals and cubicles. This toilet,
rather than being signed as male might be colour-coded
with an internationally recognisable symbol (for the
colour-blind) such as the sword and shield of Mars in (say)
blue. Persons with a vagina, irrespective of their social
expression of gender, might use a toilet containing only
cubicles colour-coded with the similarly recognisable
symbol of the hand mirror of Venus in (say) pink.
Everyone, irrespective of their social expression of gender,
would be welcome to use a third type of toilet (containing
only cubicles) colour-coded with both symbols
superimposed in (say) green.

It's not a perfect solution but if it means we can declare
at least a temporary truce on the toilet wars and focus
instead on mutual understanding, raising self-esteem and
preventing suicide, then I would wholeheartedly
recommend giving it a chance. These three types of toilet
could then be referred to solely by colour. We might have
to restrain our more enthusiastic colleagues from

demanding them in all colours of the rainbow. Institutional budgets only stretch so far!

The next chapter continues with the topic of identity – and the ethical conflicts, and spiritual resources, involved in the struggle to assume it and to change it.

17 – Dynamism and decadence

Christians, feminists and activists, trans or not, can all struggle with the honesty required by oppositional ethics. For anyone whose identity is based on resistance to a seemingly overpowering, ubiquitous and ever-increasing opposite power of domination (secularism, gender theory, abortion, homosexuality, patriarchy, kyriarchy, gender essentialism, transgenderism, homophobia, transphobia and misogyny being only some examples) there is the constant temptation to make truth the servant of strategy.

So the Vatican was censored by historians around the world when the newly-discovered Dead Sea Scrolls were whisked away and consulted only in secret. Now published (although who can guarantee that all escaped censorship?) their revelations of the daily life and dogmas of religious sects around the time of the mission of Jesus of Nazareth are presented in a theological context which doesn't rock the ideological boat.[77] Moral panic has been averted.

This kind of caution may appear both dishonest and overly dramatic, but anyone who remembers the furore caused by the publication of *The DaVinci Code* – whose author *clearly* stated that it was a work of fiction – would be at least somewhat sympathetic to the motivation: to keep quiet about new evidence that might disturb the faithful and cause them to radically question their identity, until such time as it may be presented couched in explanations that would affirm rather than disrupt that identity. Similar accusations, and similar silencing, have happened around the historical activities of the Inquisition.

---

[77] See Alexander & Alexander (2002/539) for disclaimers as to the disruptive significance of both the Dead Sea Scrolls and the Gospel of Thomas to the traditional understanding of Christianity.

The same could be said, conversely, about the dishonesty of proclaiming a woman's right to choose birth for her baby or abortion for her *foetus*, when even pro-choice feminists point out that the language used to describe life in a woman's womb varies according to whether that life is valued (principally by her) or not.[78] The related feminist silencing of women whose experience of abortion has been at best ambiguous, and at worst deeply distressing, can also be understood in that these accounts threaten one of the four core goals of Second Wave feminism: abortion on demand.[79]

So it is unsurprising that statistics on desisting and detransitioning are questioned and the kinds of harms of hormonal and surgical gender transition which Jeffreys (2014/62-79) denounces are so shouted down by transgender people and their advocates. I am quite aware that even by including work by Jeffreys in my bibliography, let alone citing her words, I am making myself vulnerable to the charge of transphobia.

So let's try to understand all this censorship. Margaret Thatcher, infamously, once said that, 'Some things can never be revealed'. Why would the Roman Catholic *Magisterium* (teaching body), feminists and transactivists appear to agree with her?

If you sincerely believe that your words, actions and the lack of either can decide the eternal bliss or torture of other souls; the local and global safety from abuse and freedom from male domination of women; or the shoring-up of self-esteem sufficient to stop a person in gender transition from committing suicide, then surely the situation may call for more flexible ethics – including censorship.

---

[78] See Wolf/1995.
[79] See McManus/2015b.

Fear of the effect of views being aired that may affect the self-esteem of already vulnerable people may partially explain some of the reaction to the radical feminist critiques of gender theory. The blogger by the name of Fire in my Belly details this reaction by publishing an 'open statement from 37 radical feminists from five countries' entitled *Forbidden Discourse: The Silencing of Feminist Criticism of "Gender"*.[80]

The statement clearly excludes male to female transsexual people from the category of women and mentions men's rights groups only negatively. To take the latter point first, the statement claims that these groups demanded to be included in the London Rad Fem conference of 2013. As a man who has both set up and participated in men's groups (but not men's rights groups) I find this demand both extraordinary and inexplicable.

The statement details threats of violence – including rape, murder and arson – made by men's rights groups and 'queer activists' against the organisers of this feminist conference as well as against a sister organisation named Deep Green Resistance (which has a similar but not identical ideology). It also reports similar threats received by other such conferences in the USA, Canada and the UK – which then have had their contracted locations cancelled by venue management groups due to fear of reprisals. This has also affected bookshops carrying publications containing these views (or on other subjects but authored by organisations which hold these views).

Given all this, it is amazing that the rest of the statement attempts to provide a balanced view of gender theory, including the shared agenda of critique of sex roles.

---

[80] Statement published 12th August 2013 on
www.feministuk.wordpress.com (accessed 6th June 2017).

Silencing and censorship are not the only choices. Another is in agreement with the Biblical injunction that 'the truth will set us free' (John 8:32). However a radical commitment to honesty is rare and risky. Let us look now at the risks that a person in gender transition faces, risks which unsympathetic criticism (from Christians or Second Wave feminists) may only make harder to face honestly.

Gender transition is a form of alchemy, a praeternatural and holistic paradigm of change.[81] This change is certainly socio-personal and may affect biological, and intellectual (and some would say also spiritual) well-being. It also involves an assumption of identity that demands huge on-going personal investment and the support of others. Let's think about what is gained and what is lost.

Dynamic Quality is, for Pirsig, the risky evolutionary impetus for change for the better that operates on all levels of reality, breaking up static patterns of value in an effort to reach a state of well-being that is even better. Sometimes it doesn't work. Although the aim is ethical, indeed moral, it doesn't feel that way for those affected by the disruption. It feels decadent and immoral.[82]

So the outrage of Christians over lost general acceptance of distinct binary gender roles; the grief of family and intimate partners; the fear of educators, youth workers and medical professionals regarding future litigation by a detransitioning or desisting adult over their part in enabling 'child abuse'; and the fury of Second Wave feminists over a man attempting to become a woman, and claiming to have always been one, or *vice-versa*, is understandable.

---

[81] See *Alchemy at the Chalkface: Pirsig, Pedagogy and the Metaphysics of Quality* (McManus/2011) for my understanding of this paradigm of change.
[82] See Pirsig/1992/126-127.

In the face of all this opposition, from people who may bitterly oppose each other on other issues (such as homosexuality and abortion) but are united on this one, it really matters to a person in gender transition that the transition not only is successful *but is clearly acknowledged to be so.*

One way of describing such transition is that a man or woman (a boy or a girl) with (about to have) a fertile body, of an outward appearance coherent with his or her anatomy, physiology and social role, ends up scarred and sterile, with an outward appearance incoherent with his or her anatomy, physiology or social role (or some part of those); the transition takes years and appearance is dependent on constant application of possibly carcinogenic levels of hormones; even after all that effort, there's no guarantee either of social, romantic or personal acceptance of the change.[83] The low self-esteem that prompted the transition may have been rendered even lower by its outcome.

Another description is that a man or woman (a boy or a girl) trapped in (terrified by the prospect of acquiring) a body incoherent with his or her real self, ends up liberated, with an outward appearance more coherent with his or her real self; the transition takes years and is risky but worth it.

---

[83] See Califia/1997/268-270 on 'the many shortcomings of SRS [sex reassignment surgery]' including disappointing neovaginal depth and neopenile/ neoclitoral function (*op. cit.*/270). The topic of 'transgender/ gender transition/ sex change regret' is both painful to those who experience it and ideologically fraught for those who see their wellbeing as threatened by its publication. See Walt Heyer's 'Regret Isn't Rare: The Dangerous Lie of Sex Change Surgery's Success' (2016) at www.thepublicdiscourse.com/2016/06/17166 *vs* Brynn Tannehill's 'Myths About Transition Regrets' (2016) at www.m.huffpost.com/us/entry/6160626

The risk of suicide is averted and the low self-esteem that prompted the transition has, finally, been raised.[84]

This book is my attempt to allow the people who hold these opposing views, or less extreme varieties, to talk to each other meaningfully. In that difficult conversation, let us remember the huge investment we have made in our own identities, and the peer support that we may take for granted in maintaining them. Let us remember also how our identities open doors or close them, how exhilarating it may have been for us to choose to assume them and how lost we might feel if we had to abandon them and become someone else unrecognisable or unacceptable to ourselves and to those we hold dear. Think, for a moment, of all the words that describe your identity most clearly. Reverse them. How would it feel to be that person? Truthfully.

Then think about this: if you wouldn't impose a religion or ideology on a child, why would you impose a gender? What about a set of clothes? Or toys? Or books? Or a language? Conversely: if you are aware of the formation of patterns of values in your child, wouldn't you want to identify and nurture them? Are you attempting to opt out of a responsibility that you already have to be a mentor?

Revisiting my summary of these twin debates, the language I used in my introduction should make more sense now:

What these two debates have in common is that on one side of each there is an assertion of a reality inaccessible to, and independent of, the evidence of the five human senses; on the other side of each there is an assertion of the distinction between symbol, similarity and identity.

---

[84] See Margaret Deirdre O'Hartigan, cited in Califia/1997/261, on naming sex-change not as transgender but as empowerment and 'shapeshift[ing]' (O'Hartigan/1993/20).

For bread and wine to be revalued as the Body and Blood of Christ, it is not necessary for Christians to believe that the atoms and molecules change; for a man to find freedom from the constraints of socially constructed masculinity, or a woman from femininity, it is not necessary that transactivists believe that chromosomes or genes change. Yet, what is revalued – in this metaphysics in which all things have value and all are held in being by intersubjective relations – is changed and changed utterly.

The ludic level of the quantum realm upon which our physical reality is based is beyond our comprehension as much as the heights of mysticism. Who can say what fleeting and ephemeral, or lasting, change our very consciousness may effect on those ever-changing unpatterned levels of reality? Shall we ever get to the point where we can truly map the routes of connection between mind and matter?

The spiritual level of reality is only comprehensible by faith – and for Christians to accept that the Eucharist occasions the possibility of an encounter between believer and Risen Lord is no great scandal. No-one has ever suggested seriously that souls are gendered and the passages of the Bible that speak of Heavenly life transcending the gender arrangements pertaining on Earth would support the view that praying 'as a man' or 'as a woman' is a socio-personal, not a spiritual, phenomenon.

Intellectually, we may always strive to find more accommodating and elegant philosophical solutions to our problematic description of holistic realities of presence and change that will always ultimately escape absolute expression. Socially, we may simply accept that different individuals and groups of people ascribe different meanings to the same phenomena. We may war with one another, attempting to force the cherished view of ourselves or our peer group upon an unwilling interlocutor – or we may see different aspects of the same phenomena reflected in a variety of description.

Described in the metaphysics I have presented here, both the pious claim of change and presence in the Eucharist and the personal and political claim of change and presence in transgender may be accorded a reality.

This is not to say that these claims are either coherent with all levels of reality or mandatory for all observers. We perceive what we value; we value what we perceive.[85] Therefore, as Eucharistic theology has attempted to avoid physicalism, transactivism may also. There is no need to claim that the host bleeds when bitten or that the bite of each communicant causes the Lord of all creation to suffer. This view was long ago condemned (see Schillebeeckx/1968).

So too, there is no need for either sterility or mental instability to be imposed by the State as a prerequisite for registration of a change of gender – as is currently the case (see Transgender Europe/2017). The biological and intellectual levels of reality are not the same as the socio-personal and if they are found to be incoherent then this metaphysics clearly explicates that this was ever so. Each level of reality may be supported by the one below but each, simultaneously, attempts to appropriate the others.

If I suddenly state that 'I am a vegan', this socio-personal resolve to be meat, fish and dairyfree and this assumption of identity has nothing whatsoever to do either with the contents of my stomach or with the coherence of my geo-political analysis of the effect on the food chain –

---

[85] See McManus/2011/163-170 on perception and value.

although, if my lapses into eating forbidden foods are too numerous, people may start to question my performance of this identity. Obviously, eating vegan supports my claim!

If I state that 'I have always been a vegan', *really*, then those who have witnessed me chomping into steak or cheesecake may have problems accepting this assertion. But I may counter that my physical and mental unease at eating animal products for years, and my harmonious lifestyle now, argue that my self-perception has validity. If the vegan identity is more to do with action than state of being, the example of nationality may fit better.

In this comparison, race is to nationality as sex is to gender. If I, as an anatomic male (presumed to be a genetic male) with monochrome light pink skin, blue eyes, a pointy nose and big ears, born in Glasgow, Scotland and brought up as a boy, identifying now as a man, now decide that I am, *really*, Nigerian, then the process of acquiring citizenship should not have to include pumping me full of Melanin, cropping my ears, flattening my nose and transplanting my eyes. Nationality does not depend upon race, even where one race is in the majority – despite this normative assumption. The world is changing.

Citizenship is a socio-personal, not a biological, pattern of values. As such, it makes little sense for me to back up my claim, to be Nigerian *really*, as part of this socio-personal transition, by stating that I have always been Nigerian. The only sense that can be made of this extraordinary statement is that, personally, I've always identified with the citizens of this country.

If I have, personally, always (or at least from an early age) made this identification and if I am known to have made it and if those who have known me for years have always agreed with this self-identification – and if

Nigerian citizens recognise me, and have always recognised me) as one of their own, even though I'm White, then this retroactive claim – even before the paperwork is complete – assumes more validity. This validity need not depend on drastic surgical intervention and is akin to that of common law marriage: by habit and repute. It's about what I value and how I am valued.

When a priest or minister echoes the words of Christ and pronounces 'this is my body', there is the possibility of a meaningful experience of the celebrant and the communicant based on values that are not confined to the spiritual level of reality. When a transgender person asserts that they are their preferred gender, *really*, there is the possibility of a meaningful experience of both speaker and listener based on values that are not confined to the socio-personal level of reality.

In other words, variously understood, there is truth in these claims to reality – even where this truth is not accessible to the five human senses. I do believe that the truth will set us free. I believe that the value we ascribe to our choice and assumption of self-defining identity may allow us to understand those of others – even though some aspects of those valued identities may clash. I believe that the transition to truth is the riskiest and most worthwhile change we can make as human beings.

To make that transition we need to commit to telling our truth courageously, to listening to the truth of others respectfully and sympathetically, to search among the rich resources of our traditions to find language that is hospitable to the perhaps alien concepts of our interlocutors, and in this real presence and real change, to encounter each other in love.

Bibliography

Alexander, Pat & Alexander, David (2002) *The Lion Handbook to the Bible*. Oxford: Lion.

Bass, Ellen & Davis, Laura (1997) *The Courage to Heal: A Guide for Women Survivors of Child Sex Abuse*. London: Vermilion.

Beemyn, Genny & Rankin, Susan (2011) *The Lives of Transgender People*. New York: Columbia University Press.

Bell, Howard H. (1996) 'Negro Nationalism in the 1850s' in *The Journal of Negro Education* www.journalnegroed.org accessed 6th September 2007 (pp.100-104).

Bell, Shannon (1993) 'Kate Bornstein: A Transgender Transsexual Postmodern Tiresias' in Arthur & Marilouise Kroker (Eds) *The Last Sex: Feminism and Outlaw Bodies*. London: MacMillan, Culture Texts, pp. 104–120.

Bennett, Susan (1997) *Theatre Audiences: A Theory of Production and Reception*. London : Routledge.

Boehner, Philotheus & Laughlin, M. Frances (Eds) (1955) *The works of Saint Bonaventure*. Saint Bonaventure, NY: Franciscan Institute, Saint Bonaventure University.

Bornstein, Kate (1994) *Gender Outlaw: On Men, Women and the Rest of Us*. New York & London: Routledge.

Broadie, Alexander (1990) *The Tradition of Scottish Philosophy: A New Perspective on the Enlightenment*. Edinburgh: Polygon.

123

Broadie, Alexander (1995) *The shadow of Scotus: philosophy and faith in pre-Reformation Scotland.* Edinburgh: T. & T. Clarke.

Burtt, E.A (1999) *The Metaphysical Foundations of Modern Physical Science.* Amherst, NY: Prometheus.

Butler, Judith (1993) *Bodies that Matter: on the discursive limits of 'sex'.* New York & London: Routledge.

Butler, Judith (1999) *Gender Trouble: Feminism and the Subversion of Identity.* New York & London: Routledge.

Califia, Pat (1997) *Sex Changes: The Politics of Transgenderism.* San Francisco, CA: Cleis Press.

Clement of Alexandria, Saint (1919) *Clement of Alexandria* (Trans. G.W. Butterworth) London: W. Heinemann; New York: G.P. Putnam's Sons.

Eco, Humberto (1984) *Postscript to the Name of the Rose.* San Diego, CA: Hardcourt Brace Jovanovich.

Edelstein, David (2016) '*Author: The JT LeRoy Story* Explores the Phenomenon of a Genuine Phony'. www.vulture.com/2016/09/movie-review-author-th-jt-leroy-story.html accessed 23rd April 2017.

Dawkins, Richard (2007) *The God Delusion.* London: Black Swan.

Davis, Georgiann (2015) *Contesting Intersex: The Dubious Diagnosis.* New York & London: New York University Press.

Fillion, Aloisius Claudies (Ed) (1887) *Biblia Sacra Juxta Vulgate (Exemplaria et Correctoria Romana). Parisiis: Sumptibus Letouzey et Ané, Editorum.*

Fine, Benny & Fine, Rafi (2012) 'Teens React to Slender', *The Fine Brothers on You Tube.* www.youtube.com accessed 20th January 2014.

Fire in my Belly (2013) *Forbidden Discourse: The Silencing of Feminist Criticism of "Gender": An open statement from 37 radical feminists from five countries'.* www.feministuk.wordpress.com (accessed 6th June 2017).

Foucault, Michel (1990) *The History of Sexuality*, Vol. I (trans. Robert Hurley) London: Vintage.

Francis, Pope (2016) *Amoris Laetitia (The Joy of Love): Apostolic Exhortation on Love in the Family.* London: Catholic Truth Society.

Gatens, Moria (1991) *Feminism and Philosophy: Perspectives on Difference and Equality.* Cambridge (UK): Polity Press.

Gell-Mann, Murray (1994) *The Quark and the Jaguar: Adventures in the Simple and the Complex.* London: Little, Brown.

Gaudenzi, Paula & Ortega, Francisco (2012) '*O estatuo da medicalização e as interpretações de Ivan Illich e Michel Foucault como ferramentas conceituais para o estudio da desmedicalização*' ['The statue of medicalization and the interpretations of Ivan Illich and Michel Foucault as conceptual tools for studying demedicalization'] in *Interface (Botucatu)* Vol 16, No. 40 Botucatu Jan./Mar. pp.21-34.

Haraway, Donna (1993) 'A Cyborg Manifesto' in Simon During (Ed.) *The Cultural Studies Reader*. London: Routledge, pp.314-336.

Hetherington, Kevin (2000) *New Age Travellers: Vanloads of Uproarious Humanity*. London & New York: Cassell.

Jarrett, James L. (Ed.) (1969) *The Educational Theories of the Sophists*. Columbia University, NY: Teachers College Press.

Jeffreys, Sheila (2014) *Gender Hurts: A feminist analysis of the politics of transgenderism*. London & New York: Routledge.

Jeremias, Joachim (1966) *The Eucharistic Words of Jesus* (Trans. Norman Perrin) London: SCM Press.

Jones, Alexander (Ed) (1968) *The Jerusalem Bible* (popular edition). London: Darton, Longman & Todd.

Kemmler, Fritz (1998) 'Entrancing "tra(u)ns/c": Some Metamorphoses of 'Transformation, Translation, and Transubstantiation'', in Carol Poster & Richard Utz (Eds) *Translation, Transformation and Transubstantiation in the Late Middle Ages* (*Disputatio* Vol. 3). Evanston, Illinois: Northwestern University Press, pp.176-222.

Marsh, Bill (2007) *Plagiarism: Alchemy and Remedy in Higher Education*. Albany, NY: State University of New York Press.

McDonnell, K. (1967) *John Calvin, the Church and the Eucharist*. Princeton, MA: Princeton University Press.

McManus, Alan (2011) *Alchemy at the Chalkface: Pirsig, Pedagogy and the Metaphysics of Quality*. Glasgow: Alan McManus.

McManus, Alan (2013) *Only Say The Word: Affirming Gay and Lesbian Love*. Arlesford (Hants): Christian Alternative.

McManus, Alan (2015a) *Dreaming Anarchy: a Shut-Eye View of a Utopia*. Glasgow: Alan McManus.

McManus, Alan (2015b) *Life Choice: the Ethics and Ideologies of Abortion*. Glasgow: Alan McManus.

McManus, Alan (2016) *Masculum et Feminam: 'Time for Inclusive Education' and the conservative Catholic*. Glasgow: Alan McManus.

Menn, Stephen (1998) *Descartes and Augustine*, Cambridge: Cambridge University Press.

Midgley, Mary (1992) *Science as Salvation: A Modern Myth and its Meaning*. London: Routledge.

Northrop, F.S.C. (1946) *The Meeting of East and West: An Inquiry Concerning World Understanding*. New York: MacMillan.

Moloney SJ, Raymond (1995) *The Eucharist*. London: G. Chapman.

More, Kate & Whittle, Stephen (Eds) (1999) *Reclaiming Genders: Transsexual Grammars at the Fin de Siècle*. London & New York: Cassell.

O'Donovan, Gerard (2017) '*Transgender Kids: Who Knows Best?* An even-handed look at gender dysphoria, review'. www.telegraph.co.uk accessed 23rd April 2017.

O'Hartigan, Margaret Deirdre (1993) 'Changing Sex Is Not Changing Gender', in *Sound Out*.

Oluo, Ijeoma (2017) 'The Heart of Whiteness: Ijeoma Oluo Interviews Rachel Dolezal, the White Woman who Identifies as Black'. www.thestranger.com accessed 23rd April 2017.

Pirsig, Robert M. (1999) *Zen and the Art of Motorcycle Maintenance: An Inquiry into Values*. London: Vintage.

Pirsig, Robert M. (1992) *Lila: An Inquiry into Morals*. London: Black Swan.

Powell, John (2010) *How Music Works: A listener's guide to harmony, keys, broken chords, perfect pitch and the secrets of a good tune.* London: Penguin.

Prosser, Jay (2006) 'Judith Butler: Queer Feminism, Transgender, and the Transubstantiation of Sex'. In Susan Stryker & Stephen Whittle (Eds) *The Transgender Studies Reader*. New York & London: Routledge, pp.257-280.

Raymond, Janice (Ed.) (1994) *The Transsexual Empire: The Making of the She-Male*. New York & London: Teachers College Press.

Ratzinger, Joseph *et al.* (1995) *Catechism of the Catholic Church* (pocket edition). London: Geoffrey Chapman.

Rilliet, Jean (1964) *Zwingli: third man of the Reformation* (trans. Harold Knight). London: Lutterworth Press.

Rose, Steve (2016) 'JT LeRoy unmasked: the extraordinary story of a modern literary hoax'. www.theguardian.com/film/2016/jul/20/jt-leroy-story-modern-literary-hoax- accessed 23rd April 2017.

Ross, W.D. (1924) *Αριστοτελουσ Τα Μετα Τα Φυσικα (Aristotle's Metaphysics): A Revised Text with Introduction and Commentary.* Vol. 1, Oxford: Clarendon Press.

Samson, Geoffrey (1997) *Educating Eve: The 'Language Instinct' Debate.* London & New York: Cassell.

Schillebeeckx O.P., Edward (1968) *The Eucharist* (trans. N.D. Smith) London & Sydney: Sheed and Ward.

Selin Davis, Lisa (2017) 'My Daughter Is Not Transgender. She's a Tomboy'. *The New York Times.* www.nytimes.com accessed 25th April 2017.

Shankman, Paul (2009) *The Trashing of Margaret Mead: Anatomy of an Anthropological Controversy.* Madison, Wisconsin: The University of Wisconsin Press

Sokolowski, Robert (2006) *Christian Faith & Human Understanding: Studies of the Eucharist, Trinity, and the Human Person.* Washington, DC: The Catholic University of America Press.

Souter, Alexander (Ed) (1941) *Novvm Testamentvm Graece. Oxon: E Typographeo Clarendoniano.*

Stallings, Joseph (c.1988) *Rediscovering Passover.* San Jose, CA: Resource Publications.

Tarrant, Shira (2006) *When Sex Became Gender.* New York & London: Routledge.

Transgender Europe (2017) 'The Momentum is now! Forced sterilisation is on its way out, but trans pathologisation remains'. Available at www.tgeu.org/idahot_forum_map_launch/ accessed 24th May 2017.

Wolf, Naomi (1995) 'Our Bodies, Our Souls: Rethinking Pro-choice Rhetoric,' in *The New Republic*, October 16, pp.26-35.

Whittle, Stephen (2002) *Respect and Equality: Transsexual and Transgender Rights.* London; Sydney; Portland, Oregon: Cavendish.

THE RULER

A cautionary tale

April was proud of her 9.82 Personal Commensurability Average. Her name was not, in fact, the caprice that it seemed: The Ruler had shown that Galvanic Skin Nurture Response was markedly higher among gen-Fems who chose idiosyncratic appellations for their offspring. Her third-parent's generation had, after the Great Commensuration, universally adopted numbers until the GSNR figures were collated and the Ruler also showed that citizen identification accuracy increased by up to 50% when appellation and Rep-Id were non-identical.

All this information was to be found in *Lifestyle*, the Fem-mag which, as well as showing weekly statistics, featured Paradigm Interview, in which a citizen would show how it maintained a high PCA. April, (50Cy, Fem, neg5cm, 50% Melanin, hair-shade3, eye-shade4) was both gene and nurture-mother to two offspring: May and June. May (12Cy) was Fem and had already celebrated her Gender-Day; June (8Cy) was born Hom but April felt that it may choose not to identify as gen-Hom but rather as gen-Fem when its Day came. April told the interviewer that she considered the similarity between gen-Hom and gen-Free apparel sensible, as she wanted June to be able to consider choosing the latter.

The interviewer was surprised at this observation and put it down to Media Attention Stress (on first interview varying by up to 20% from a mean of 700 Galvanic Skin Stress Response) and quoted statistics of pre-gen Gender Anxiety level showing a decline to roughly a quarter for those young citizens who choose to identify as gen-Free. *Lifestyle* recorded the Ruler-Reference.

The rest of the interview was taken up by April recounting aspects of her Lifestyle: trading, domicility, pedagogy and dating. April's current date was a Hom stat-worker, co-incidentally the gene-father of June, and the interviewer gave her positive verbal affirmation on their Companionship CA and noted that April's Neuro-Linguistic Response changed considerably after the affirmation. *Lifestyle* quoted statistics of falls averaging 70% of N-L Stress after reception of verbal positive affirmation – as compared to graphic (being 50%) – and gave the Ruler-Reference.

The interviewer was especially interested in April's function as a pedagogue. April said she enjoyed working in Junior-Academy and that, as it was the nearest to her offspring's dwelling, she was lucky enough to educate both May and June. The interviewer reminded her that the laws of chance are incommensurate and changed the subject to that of Kinaesthetic Learning in Mixed Ability/Age Groups and quoted statistics showing far higher Personal and Group CA among pre-gens than in control groups. April agreed with her.

Back home, April infused some Herb-calm, downloaded the mag and settled back on her recliner to read it. The sun was setting and she enjoyed watching the colours: 1, 1.5, 2 and the darker clouds of 6. The bay was beautiful with sailboats – and she saw that there was an article entitled Sailing and Stress Reduction but she wanted to read her interview first, she was sure her N-L Stress had been above average.

It was as she remembered, except that she felt it was shorter. She had enjoyed the interview, her first, and supposed that it had been edited for word length. The facing article was a discussion on Rep-lexis, in which a gen-Free pointed out that the lexical item "pre-gen" was felt in fact to be incommensurate with the gender choice of gen-Free which was to choose no gender at all. A recent opinion-poll carried out by *Freestyle* was inconclusive – there being no clear vote margin between those who considered the particle 'Free' in the lexical item 'gen-Free' to be the predicate of 'gen' or to be adjective-intransitive.

The question was, therefore, whether 'gen-Free' designated a choice of gender or a refusal of gender category. Further to the question of gender was the consideration that if 'Free' is identified as a gender (and not a refusal of such) with 'Fem' and 'Hom'; then, as the latter two are strictly applied only to citizens with those Birth Gender Characteristics (those with other BGCs choosing these genders identifying as 'gen-Fem' and 'gen-Hom') then citizens of both hermaphrodite and neuter BGCs are effectively lumped in together.

The citizen made it clear that this was not an accusation of Akrasia – neither imputed to the Ruler as a whole or any stat-worker in particular (given that collation of clear statistics on these questions was inconclusive even among the 'Free'/gen-Free community) – and invited readers of both *Lifestyle* and *Farmstyle* to come up with suggestions (either philosophical or lexical) to aid greater commensurability.

This was the kind of challenge that April enjoyed – although Augustus didn't like to discuss that sort of thing, having enough of it at work – and she pondered these questions as she cooked her vegetable stir-fry and rice. The Mensa was always open but after she had read that self-cooking lowers N-L Stress by an amazing 80% (if dates, siblings, parents or offspring are not present) she had started to cook by herself and during the day looked forward to the time of thinking things over.

She would go to bed after the recommended two hours post-feeding and, with no work to prepare for the morrow, watched stat-docs on the visor to fill in the time. At eighty-clock the Evening Admonition came on and she adopted the Reverential Posture and repeated the words with the presenter on screen:

All things are within Reason's grasp,
All things are ruled by the Ruler,
The Ruler keeps us from Akrasia,
My body, my mind, my thoughts, my deeds,
All these are commensurable.

Just as she was drifting off to sleep, April remembered what it was that had been cut out of the interview. It was their discussion on luck, chance, and incommensurability.

...

April awoke to the quiet but persistent beep of the chron-waker. She ached all over and was reluctant to get out of bed. About twelve-clock her moon-time had started and she had got up to put on a Fem-pad and take elixir. Although she had now slept for a further eighteen chrons, she still felt exhausted. She switched off her calor-pack and rubbed her abdomen with a groan. In her bath (adjusted +10Body-Heat, with added Fem-therapy) she tried to think positively about the day ahead. She had been looking forward to her Rep-Ed day but would now have to ask for substitution.

In fact she didn't have to – there were no rules, only guidelines – but the alternative was to go out in public wearing her colour1 moon-badge and have everything she did logged for her to re-confirm the next day. She remembered that on Afternoon Forum today representatives from all three Style-mags would be

135

showing how they envisaged colour-schemes and ergonomics in three identical personal dwellings. Usually the gradual transformation over ten days (from empty box of walls, floors, ceilings and roof) excited April but today she felt she couldn't get excited about anything.

Crunching through her first-meal grain, sitting at the food-board, April glanced at her diary and saw that tonight she had booked a date with Augustus. The last time they'd had a date he'd stayed the night and she wasn't sure if that was reasonable this time. This morning, looking for Fempads in the bathroom, she'd found his Rep-Id Card. It had slipped down the side of the calor-unit (fortunately switched off as it was Second Season). It must have fallen from his apparel when he took it off to bathe before mating. She pressed his photo-icon on her talker.

"Good morning Citizen, how may I assist you?"

"Good morning Citizen, may I talk with Hom Augustus?"

"Speaking, Fem April," he'd had time to verify the voice-print, "how nice to talk with you and how are you today? I'm very much looking forward to our date tonight and I wondered if you'd like to try something special?"

"Hom Augustus, honey, actually I'm on my moon-time and I wondered if you'd like to meet for third-meal somewhere and then watch a Rep-doc? I need an early night."

"Oh. Well in that case I won't disturb you. Let's book Saturn-day night?"

"Oh but we could still…"

"No, no, a colleague in Companionship showed me stats the other day of a 75% decline in CA for moon-time dates. Why don't you get masseur to make you feel better?

Somatic Sensuality readings show a negative co-relative to roughly 80% of N-L Stress."

"Interesting. Well thanks for the information. I'll bear it in mind."

"See you Saturn-day, hon."

"Over."

It wasn't the politest form of ending a talk – usually reference was made to a future meeting (even if a date was unspecified) – by both parties, but Fems on their moon-time had an automatic Akrasia-Waiver of 20%. Anyway, her next Therapy was Mercury-day, in four days' time, so she'd see him before and be able to score higher. She'd forgotten to tell him about his Card. Stat-workers, in fact, hardly used theirs, as they were iris-cleared on entering the Ruler and also when logging on. She was reaching again for the talker when it occurred to her that she should inform the junior-academy as early as possible, to facilitate substitution.

"Good morning, Citizen, how may I assist you?"

"Hi, Free Rose, look I'm on my moon, I recognised your voice and I just wanted to hurry up and tell you that so I'm sorry I didn't give you the standard greeting and I mean no irreverence to your status…"

"Fem April, breathe."

April sighed, and laughed. "Okay maybe I should take more elixir."

"Have you already taken the recommended dose?"

"Yes."

"Then why don't you tell me what's really wrong?"

"Free Rose, you are a gem, it's just, well, I know it's irrational but…"

"You *are* on moon-time."

"It's got NOTHING to do with that! I'm sorry, I didn't mean to shout."

"That's okay, the auto-mute caught it. What's wrong, dear?"

"Well first I was so looking forward to this Rep-Ed day, the last one I did was last Cycle and now I can't go…"

Rose cleared its throat at this point and said, "Go on."

"…and I phoned Augustus because we have, had, a date tonight. I mean it should really make no difference…"

"Not according to stats," said Rose in measured tones.

"Well, that's what *he* said. He told me to get a masseur and booked another date for Saturn-day but that's two days from now! I want to see him today!" She started to cry.

"Fem April, would you like me to send you round a therapist?"

"No, no, I'm fine." April's voice was still shaky.

"Do you know what I would recommend?"

"What?"

"That you take control. Now what do you *really* want to do today?"

"I really want to do that Rep-Ed day."

"Do you feel up to it?"

"Yes. I think it would cheer me up more than watching the visor all day – or any masseur for that matter."

"Don't underestimate massage. I always get one when I have the same problem."

April was touched. It was very unusual for gen-Frees to divulge their BGCs and inquiries were never made.

"Thanks, Free Rose. I won't."

"Okay if that's what you really want, I'll now tell you that, in fact, we've had a few functionaries requesting substitution due to incapacity today and that, if you didn't go, we wouldn't be able to cover it and the citizen would have to postpone its Rep-Ed day to next Epi-Cycle. In fact, I'd be pleased if you would go because if we get another postponement our Theory-Academy CA will slip by 10%."

"In that case I'll go. Thanks Free Rose."

"And don't worry about Hom Augustus. He'll probably go to a pro-mate if he feels that way. That's what my date usually does when I'm not interested. I don't mind, I've got my garden."

"Thank-you for your assistance, Citizen, I look forward to our next meeting, tomorrow, Jupiter-day."

"Only if you feel fine, Citizen, just clip on that badge and don't worry – and get a massage, you'll love it! I am glad to have been of assistance and look forward to seeing you well!"

April smiled, said "Over," and switched off the talker. So Rose was a born-Fem! She wondered if it downloaded *Lifestyle* as well as *Freestyle*. April wondered about doing the same – it would be assumed that she did so for a date, not for herself – it might help her to understand Rose more now that it had shown such confidence in her. She might also download *Farmstyle* to help her understand Augustus. Now *there* was a thought. And with that reasoning, greater citizen comprehension, there was no reason to think such actions incommensurate.

She touched the stat-icon on the visor and it expanded to full-screen. Drawing the name and Rep-Id of the citizen she was to educate today across the screen from her diary column, she tapped it twice to give details. '40Cy, Hom, pos2cm, 30% Melanin, hair-shade2, eye-shade6' appeared on the screen, followed by stats on his current date, their CCA, recent changes in his domicility, trading and function (mechanical-hygienist) stats and his PCA, calculated this week as 4.12.

April saw that from the beginning of the Cycle there was a constant decline in all his stats but that despite frequent changes of date – and the variation which this inevitably produced – his (their) CCA was the only stat which remained anywhere near the level of PCA (7.89) which had been his average last Cycle. Therapy had recommended Rep-Ed as the stats did not seem to be in relation to psychosomatic figures (which were optimal) but rather seemed to show personal volition. Balanced against that was the consideration that, especially in terms of PCA, there was indistinction between Akrasia of Commission and Omission and Therapy felt that an educator might either solve the problem or shed more light on the stats.

...

Once outside, April had wondered whether taking on this assignment was reasonable in her condition but the thought of being boxed in all day had decided her. The metro-plane ride over the lava field was smooth and by the time she had disembarked at the Ruler she felt almost cheerful. She had put Augustus' Rep-Id Card into her holder, hoping to have time to hand it in at Reception before her student arrived but, walking in the threshold, she saw that a facilitator, accompanied by a citizen in Hom apparel – who fitted the stats she had checked at home – was coming to greet her.

"Welcome, Gen-Fem, do I have the pleasure of addressing Fem April?"

April had forgotten that the metro-pilot would have sent the passenger-stats on. She did, however remember Ruler-protocol. "Greetings, facilitator, your information is correct, I am Fem April. May I presume that I have the pleasure of addressing Hom Boron?"

The facilitator stopped momentarily, adjusting its welcome-program to accommodate April's unusual use of protocol. Educators were allowed a great deal of variation in how they conducted Rep-Ed days, student-rapport being considered 90% more effective than protocol-convention. "Your information is correct, Fem April, this citizen is Hom Boron, your student for today."

The humanoid turned its silver face to the Hom, "Hom Boron…"

"Yeah, thanks, I think I got it too, thanks all the same."

The facilitator stopped again and April tried to hide her half-smile at this almost total lack of protocol but the facilitator was already handing them passes and info-blocks which they both put in their holders then bowed to the humanoid and all gave the Valedictory together, "Reason rule your day."

The facilitator wheeled smoothly away, back to Reception, and April told the holders to lead the way, which they did, joining together and rising to hover at face height then moving off in the direction of a large arch made of a smooth stone of colour5.

Both remained silent until the gates but, having flashed their Cards at the sensor, when the field switched off and they stepped through into the Learning Zone, April turned to the Hom and smiled. "I see, Hom Boron, that you are as impatient with Ruler-protocol as I am."

The other looked at her warily.

Maybe she had been too previous. "I mean no disrespect of your status, citizen, it's simply that, as you can see, I'm on my moon-time and I wonder if you'd allow me to schedule a beverage-break before we begin Education?"

The Hom relaxed. "Of course, Fem April, I thank you for assisting me at what may perhaps be an uncomfortable time."

How charming! And he had used her appellation – a sign of close rapport in 75% of speech-interactions.

"Thank-you for your solicitude, Hom Boron," April sat down on a rest and pressed the facilitator-icon on her holder, "may I presume that you know of this discomfort from someone close?" This was risky and she wouldn't have dared if she didn't know that his current date was gen-Fem.

His face looked amused and she wondered why but just then a facilitator wheeled up and she asked for Herb-calm and he for Aquavit.

"Actually my dates have never included a Fem, my current date is a born-Hom."

Her face paled. How could she have been so stupid! "Gen-Hom, please forgive my impertinence! You are at liberty to terminate this day and postpone it until another, less rude Educator may be found." She stood up, shaken.

"Please sit down. You had no intention of offending, I'm sure. Anyway, as you say you're on your moon-time and I do know that's difficult as my nurture-mother used to tell me about it."

He winked at her and she laughed at how he had turned the tables on her.

She decided to be honest. "Hom Boron, you know I have your stats, but that information doesn't include any BGCs. I wanted to establish rapport and I made a stupid mistake."

"Well most gen-Fems are Fems."

"75%."

She could have bitten her lip but it came out automatically. She tried to remedy it with a joke, "So I suppose that makes me only 25% stupid."

He laughed. "Laureen gets *Lifestyle* and I read your interview and you come across as highly intelligent. So you don't fool me!"

She held back from quoting her IQ (98) and realised that the speech-interaction had a generally rising rapport. She also realised that he knew what she was trying to accomplish.

"Hom Boron, I won't insult your intelligence by pretending not to know why we're here today. In this Cycle your PCA and other stats (not, however, your CCA) have steadily declined. Today I expected to meet with a stubborn and negative-thinking Hom, incapable or unwilling to make reasonable personal and social choices, and instead I meet a charming, witty citizen to whom solicitude to strangers and cherishing close relationships are obvious priorities".

He stared at her without speaking for a moment and she wondered if she'd gone too far.

There was one way to find out. "Hom Boron, what's wrong?"

"You've got the Therapy report, "he said thickly.

"The conclusion reads 'the reason for this increasing level of Akrasia is, as yet, undiagnosed'." She let that sink in, then added, "Hom Boron, the only people in a rational society like the Republic who make irrational choices are those who are uninformed of current stats or incapable of comprehending them".

"And such people are cared for in the Dwellings of the Akratics." He swallowed.

"Their preferred name is the Care-Homes. Hom Boron, I don't believe that you are one of those people and I would prefer – and I'm sure you would too, not to mention all those you are close too (Gen-Fem Laureen and your nurture-mother, for instance) – that you contribute to our society and enjoy its benefits to the best of your ability."

"My nurture-mother lived her last year in one of those places." He stared straight at April, unblinking.

April had spoken another citizen's Beloved Dead, unheeding.

She bowed her head, clasped her hands and intoned, "Her Life had Reason, may we know this Reason and be ruled by it."

She looked up at him. For this fault there was neither apology nor forgiveness, she must simply bear it.

"I used to go and see her, every Sun-day, and spend all day with her. She was so happy to see me. We used to walk in the garden and when I left I would say, "Only five days till I'm back, Mother. She used to stand at the gates and wave me through the field. She'd be there when I arrived too, the next Sun-day. Then one Sun-day she wasn't."

April breathed out slowly, "May I speak of your Beloved Dead, citizen?"

"Citizen, you may."

"May I ask when your Beloved mother left her Life?"

"At the beginning of this Cycle."

"May I ask if her Mourning was according to Protocol?"

"It was."

"May I ask if I may assist you with any aspect of this Mourning?"

He was silent.

April drew breath, "Citizen, I will not…"

"There is one small thing…"

She saw that he was crying and waited.

"…her lair…"

April thought he had finished, "May I …"

"Her lair. I put some words on it – and they've taken them off."

He dissolved into sobs now and April sat quite still until he had somewhat recovered.

"Citizen, I will not speak more of your Beloved Dead. I thank you for your permission."

"Citizen, your words were apt."

The ritual response seemed to steady him and April felt she could proceed.

"Hom Boron. Thank-you for the confidence in me which the shedding of tears demonstrates," she omitted to quote the stats for lowering blood-pressure, "I will investigate – with your permission – this infringement of Mourning and report to you."

"Thank-you." He dried his eyes and April saw the opportunity for a natural (and much-needed) change of atmosphere.

"Hom Boron, would you excuse me? Perhaps you would like to start looking at the displays? I'll be with you in a minute."

He realised her necessity when she separated her holder from his, told it to seek a Fem-room and followed it hurriedly. Blushing, he turned away to look at a crystal case in the centre of the dome in which they stood.

…

When April came back, she found him looking through the crystal of the central case.

"What are these books?"

He turned and smiled, expecting her answer.

"They are surviving examples of the Seven Amusements."

"We didn't get taught in Trade-Academy about them. What are they."

"They are extremes of Akrasia, all incommensurable with Reason." April repeated the words of her pre-history educator without thinking.

He looked at her in astonishment. "But they're just books!"

Her voice was sententious, "Books such as these, in their time caused bloodshed, poverty, famine, crimes for which we no longer have names, homelessness, disease and, finally, Earthdusk."

"How could they have caused so much wrong? I thought Earth simply had an ecological disaster and our fore-parents escaped in ships, seeding clouds and cooling the lava-flows to dry land?"

April smiled, she had taught those very words to her students at Junior-Academy just yesterday morning.

"The Seven Amusements led the Earth-People to consider only the appearance of things and not their function, they encouraged deception, raised passions and madness; this first is a book of Poetry – words are ranged across the page for their effect on the ear and the sensibilities when spoken. This might seem innocuous, but especially when joined to Music – an arrangement of pleasant noises – love-sonnets and national hymns were produced, lamenting lost loves and lands and spurring to greater glories on field and in bed. Drama followed, actors representing these things – things that are false – on raised platforms for all the citizens to see and be affected, accompanied by Art which replicated images of real things on two dimensions. It is reasonable to move from the unreal toward the Real but not *vice-versa* and so all these irrational behaviours were compounded in Religion when people imagined that all their own false creation had some other source than their festering minds – and worshipped it. Media magnified these errors by promoting them all over Earth until not one corner was unaffected and finally those who tried to escape the terror by use of Allopathy found more terror awaiting them."

April paused, she hadn't meant to repeat, almost word-for-word the opening words of the first lecture of her educator so many Cycles ago. How had the words stuck in her mind?

"And all that started from Poetry?"

"Yes." She was recovering herself now, she should have more elixir soon; she could feel the pain beginning again.

"Is that why they took my words away?"

April didn't want to re-open the subject but asked carefully, "What did you write?"

He cleared his throat and declaimed:

> *To a dear, Beloved Mum,*
> *From me, your loving son,*
> *Now you lie in peace*
> *Now I cry in grief*
> *Your life had Reason*
> *And it will rule me.*

"That's so beautiful!"

"Is it Poetry?"

"Yes, unfortunately, it's Poetry…"

April stopped, a shiver running up her spine, remembering the words of the interviewer about chance and luck – and surely fortune – being incommensurate.

"Do I have your permission to suggest a small change and to request that the alternative version be replaced on…on where it was originally?"

"Okay, what?"

"Dearly Beloved Mum: Now you lie in peace here while I cry in grief at your memory. However I remember your life had Reason and it will rule me. Your loving son, Hom Boron."

"Do you think that's as good?"

"What does the first version do?"

"It makes me want to cry."

"And the second?"

"It's much more reasonable. It makes me want to buck up and get on with it."

"Hom Boron?"

"Yes?"

"Will you be able to?"

"Buck up and get on with it, reasonably?"

"Yes."

"Yes I think I will. I understand now. Thank-you, Fem April."

"Hom Boron, with your permission I will use one of these terminals here to forward this request to the Resting Place – while it's fresh in my mind."

He nodded.

"Citizen, your Republic-Education day is over, you are at liberty to view the stat-hist-docs or displays of the Dome if you wish, or you may leave. Metro-planes leave for the Polis every half-chron."

"Educator, I thank you for your assistance and I will take my leave."

They both bowed, said the Valedictory and she watched him walking through the field, he turned as he did so and, on impulse, she waved. She immediately sent the request, using the exact phrasing she had suggested to him. Then she filed her report and added a recommendation that the Lair-Keeper and all staff of the Resting-Place should copy their action-reports to Therapy and that stats should be collated on possible inverse relation between Mourning Trauma and all citizen stats, especially PCA. She logged off and stood up, with a groan. The pain was back with a vengeance now; she *must* take some elixir now. But first she lingered by the crystal case.

It was perfectly square and held the seven differently-sized books on slender titanium stands. The last time she had been here she hadn't glanced at it – the Education session had involved her helping the student to review most of its life choices (the root of the Akrasia being, as far as she could see, that it simply didn't like making choices) and she'd had no leisure to inspect the displays.

All were Pre-Commensuration and the covers faded but the plasma labels named their authors: Liz Lochhead; Holst; Calderón de la Barca; Janet A. Kaplan; Kramer & Sprenger; Glasgow Media Group; Irvine Welsh.

"Dreaming Frankenstein, The Planets Suite, La Vida es Sueño, Unexpected Journeys: The Art and Life of Remedios Varo, Mallaeus Maleficarum, Bad News, Trainspotting," she shivered as she read out the names – those she could understand sounded horrible and she knew they all were. She walked round the case, heading for the gate, surveying the backs of the books and the blurb on the poetry-book caught her eye:

Human relationships, especially as seen from a woman's point of view, are central: attraction, pain, acceptance, loss, triumphs and deceptions; always made immediate through her imagery and acute powers of observation and through her flair as a storyteller.

Woman, she thought, *the archaic name for 'Fem'. Or gen-Fem? No, didn't they punish gender-shift? This book must be like* Lifestyle. *Dangerous though.* She read the blurb again and involuntarily thought of Augustus, and Rose's assumption that he would go to a pro-mate.

But she didn't feel pain, his behaviour was only reasonable – and she might get that massage after all, it was a good idea. There was nothing to connect her with this 'woman' from a planet that had destroyed itself. But she was curious; and the sun (slowly rising on this side of the world as it was still setting on the Polis) poured down through the translucent curvature of the Dome and April felt suddenly that everything was very still.

She watched her hands approach the holder and extract Augustus' Card. She watched her hands turn it over so that its genetic fingerprint bar hovered over the lock-cell of the case. She heard a soft whirr and a mute click as the crystal side nearest her wavered and disappeared. She felt her fingers enclose the book of Poetry and slide to open it.

April,
April first you must fool me
I am no longer
anybody's fool.[86]

---

[86] 'Memo to Myself for Spring' in 'Memo for Spring' in Liz Lochhead (1984) *Dreaming Frankenstein & Collected Poems*. Edinburgh: Polygon Books, pp.158-159.

She smiled at seeing her own name, but it was only a coincidence, like all those that had happened today. And Poetry was the least of the Amusements – only the first really and even Hom Boron had written poetry, unintentionally, and had meant no harm, nor done none. And she would only read a little more then shut it and put it away forever and no-one would ever know – it would be her secret.

The next lines were about dancing and religion! And what could it mean that a 'man' (Hom) was 'velvet-tongued'? She tried simultaneously to imagine and to drive the half-formed images from her brain. 'Plaster statues'?

She felt her fear rising and her hands trembled as they gripped the book. She saw pictures in her mind, pictures that this Fem/ woman must have seen, must have wanted her to see, speaking to her across space, across generations. She could not stop now. The next lines were about hope, and guarding against it.

But she could not stop the rise of hope in her, that here was some answer, overlooked, to questions only her body asked because her mind had no words to frame them.

The following lines made no sense. Why was March mad? What did it mean? And wasn't 'put out' an archaic and derogatory lexical reference to mating? What was the link with charity? Another unreasonable, and unjust, archaic Earth custom.

April laughed, unreasonably, because she did not understand the joke, but the words jolted her and rhymed in her head and she read on, regardless.

These next lines were hardly read before they transported her to cosmetic counters. At least she knew what they were. This 'woman' was speaking to her!

There were no stats here, no facts, no rules, no numbers; yet April felt the thrill of the truth of this poem, this funny sequence of words that tickled her ears as she read them out into the golden light of the Dome.

She knew these urges, this rising hope and fancy. This was a crazy idea. A whim. Just as well she was on her moon. She breathed out; no-one had spotted her lingering by the open crystal case. There was only the last four lines left. April would close the book and never look at it again. This was her last moment of reading Poetry. Her last. Forever.

> *But April first you must fool me.*
> *April,*
> *I fear you*
> *May*

She knew it was the beginning of Akrasia, she knew it was incommensurate with Reason, she knew that this was the reason why Earth was dead and its Moon a graveyard of star battleships and military bases. She knew that numbers and not passions ruled the Universe, that Tragedy followed unmeasured feelings, that each human need had to be reckoned one against the other until their conflict was cancelled and only utility remained.

But as she pressed this book against her heart, as she felt its beat and the words accompany her rhythm and the golden light of the Dome pulse with it and the whole building of the Ruler and all within, and the lava plain surrounding and the round mass of Zuhra, (four point eight six nine times ten to the power of twenty-four kilogrammes, second planet from the benevolent Sun) upon which she stood, rushing round in its perfect orbit; she felt, although it could not be true, that she heard Music.

THE END[87]

_____

[87] Statistics on Venus from Michael E. Bakich (2000) *The Cambridge Planetary Handbook*. Cambridge (UK): Cambridge University Press.

Afterword – homage to Robert M. Pirsig

Towards the end of the writing of this book I received the news that Dr Robert M. Pirsig, bestselling author of *Zen and the Art of Motorcycle Maintenance* and *Lila*, and philosophical inspiration for my series of books on education and ethics, had died. May he rest in peace and may his good works live on. The Greeks have a wise saying for the bereaved: 'live and remember him!'

Although he saw Aristotle as a formidable philosophical opponent, a conceptual trickster responsible for much division and harm, he might be amused at the irony of his fulfilment of the peripatetic maxim that a life well-lived is known only in death. Transparent at the harm he had done to himself, and hinting at that he had done to others, whose story was not his to tell, yet Pirsig still might be an example of Aristotle's ideal of human flourishing and both he and his mentor Plato knew well the danger of celebrity (in Macedonia and Syracuse, respectively) which Pirsig, having acquired, wisely shunned.

His name, through the unreferenced misquotation of his words by Richard Dawkins, is in some quarters synonymous with a rejection of religion but it was Buddhism, not psychiatry (and certainly not electro-shock) that restored his shattered sanity and no-one can read his words without awareness of his deep appreciation for the mystical dimension of life.

I did not have the privilege of meeting him but my good friend and colleague Dr Anthony McWatt, first to complete a doctorate on Pirsig's work, met him on several occasions and corresponded frequently. That acquaintance is his to describe but I know it was characterised by a friendly and stimulating meeting of minds. I believe Pirsig was the greatest, and most misunderstood, philosopher of the 20th century and in this new century his words still have value:

> What you have to do, if you get caught in this gumption trap of value rigidity, is slow down – you're going to have to slow down anyway whether you want to or not – but slow down deliberately and go over ground that you've been over before to see if the things you thought were important were really important and to...well...just *stare* at the machine. There's nothing wrong with that. Just live with it for a while. Watch it the way you watch a line when fishing and before long, as sure as you live, you'll get a little nibble, a little fact asking in a timid, humble way if you're interested in it. That's the way the world keeps happening: be interested in it.
>
> (Pirsig/1999/311, emphasis original)

About the Author

A former Franciscan friar, Alan McManus, M.Theol. (hons), M.Phil, PGDE, M.Litt., Ph.D., is a freelance academic, novelist, playwright and dramaturg. His doctoral thesis, *Alchemy at the Chalkface: Pirsig, Pedagogy and the Metaphysics of Quality,* is on the work of the creative and contrarian American Philosopher, Dr Robert M. Pirsig.

Only Say The Word: Affirming Gay and Lesbian Love, (Christian Alternative, 2013) is first, and *Life-Choice: the Ethics and Ideologies of Abortion* the second, in a series of books based on his doctoral thesis – which also informs his booklet, *Masculum et Feminam: 'Time for Inclusive Education' and the conservative Catholic.* This thesis and his ethnographic dissertation, *Dreaming Anarchy: a Shut-Eye View of a Utopia,* are discussed in his chapter, 'Strange Attractors: Myth, Dream, and Memory in Educational Methodology', in the *International Handbook of Interpretation in Educational Research* (Springer, 2015). He has also published articles on political philosophy and WW1 remembrance in the online journal, *Citizenship, Social and Economics Education.*

His plays, *Shock Doctrine* and *Jésus de Glasgow*, have been performed by Tent City Theatre Company in various community venues in Glasgow and at the family-friendly Arts and Music festival 'Doune the Rabbit Hole'. His seven-minute radio play on dementia as subversive remembrance, *Mrs Atkins remembers*, was first broadcast on SubCity Radio, then by Philanthrobeats to mark the Christmas Truce (both on You-Tube) and is now broadcast annually on Remembrance Sunday on Sunny Govan Radio. *Redemption*, a monologue in homage to Dostoyevsky's Alyona, has been performed in Glasgow in English and Scots versions.

A slim volume of verse is forthcoming and his poem 'The Levelling' is published online and in print in the publicity for the film of that name (Hope Dickson Leach, Pecadillo Pictures, 2016).

Writing as Alan Ahrens-McManus, he has also published five books of the Bruno Benedetti Mysteries, a series of inclusive stories set in Glasgow, starting with *Tricks of the Mind* which is followed by *The Lovers*, *Shades of the Sun*, *Qismet* and *Tìr nam Bàn*.

Dear Reader

Thank-you for reading this book. Please consider reviewing *Trans/Substantitation* on your favourite online retailer and telling your friends about it in person and via social media. You can let me know about reviews through Twitter: @gumptionology

Alan

Printed in Great Britain
by Amazon